ROUTE

ROUTE 63

Around England on a Free Bus Pass

Dave Hadfield

Scratching Shed Publishing Ltd

Copyright © Dave Hadfield 2015
All rights reserved
The moral right of the author has been asserted
First published by Scratching Shed Publishing Ltd in 2015
Registered in England & Wales No. 6588772.
Registered office:
47 Street Lane, Leeds, West Yorkshire. LS8 1AP
www.scratchingshedpublishing.co.uk
ISBN: 978-0993188206

A catalogue record for this book is available from the
British Library.

Cover illustration © Mark Eastbrook
www.markeastbrook.co.uk

Inside illustrations © Sophie Hadfield

Typeset in Warnock Pro Semi Bold and Palatino
Printed and bound in the United Kingdom by
Latimer Trend & Company Ltd,
Estover Road, Plymouth, PL6 7PY

Dedicated to the country bus drivers of England, without whose skill at the wheel nobody would get very far at all. Special thanks to my GP, Dr Dharmesh Mistry, and the National Health Service, who have done more than anyone to keep me running approximately to timetable.

The Author

Dave Hadfield has been a journalist and author for almost 40 years, notably as the rugby league correspondent of *The Independent*. He has also written widely on a range of other subjects. This is his ninth book. He lives in Bolton with his wife, a variable number of children and a bus pass.

Contents

Contents

Route 63: An Explanation

WHY Route 63? The original idea for this book's title was Route 65, because it chimed with the male pension age and because of its proximity to the highway immortalised by Chuck Berry. But it wasn't on my 65th birthday that I set out into the unknown or partially known; it was on my 63rd and I wasn't adding two years to my age for anyone.

In fact, I'd already had the 'open sesame' shard of plastic for over a year before that. At one time, you got it at 60, but a sliding scale designed to harmonise eventually with women's entitlement now gives it to you some months later. In any case, I already had the disabled pass that you can get regardless of age, but that is a different story. Better to keep it simple. Route 63 it was.

I didn't set out with a lot of pre-conceived questions in mind, let alone any plans to dig out particular answers. It would just be a ramble through the back-roads, with eyes and ears open for anything that took my fancy. I had no

Route 63: An Explanation

philosophy to peddle, no theory to support; I just wanted to see the country in which I live from a different angle. Most of all, I didn't want to spend any money doing it. My publishers are Yorkshiremen and I can't begin to describe to you just how excited they were about this aspect of the game-plan.

It took just over a month, split into two journeys which, between them, took me on something very close to a full circuit of England.

I'd been fortunate in that I'd seen a lot of the country already, but not in the same way; not like some huge film loop played through the windows of more than 100 buses. I saw England at its most beautiful and at its ugliest; at its most fragile and its most resilient, at its most welcoming and its most paranoid.

It was a journey that fascinated and entertained me; that made me rejoice and, occasionally, made me despair. I'm a lucky man to have been able to do it.

For the opportunity, I have to thank Tony, Phil and Ros at Scratching Shed and our resident bus guru, Andrew Cudbertson. Between them, they kept me on the right route – most of the time, at least.

Many thanks also to Sky Sports presenter Dave Clark, who has personal experience of some of the issues raised in this book and who kindly agreed to write a foreword.

And not forgetting my youngest daughter, Sophie, who created the illustrations which weave in so effectively with the text like a 582 in heavy traffic on St Helens Road.

Foreword

Dave Clark
Sky Sports Presenter

🚌

DAVE HADFIELD and I have an awful lot in common. For starters we are both Northerners called Dave. We are both obsessed with sport, folk music and real ale. We also both happen to be lifetime members of the same exclusive club.

That club isn't a fancy gin palace in Mayfair, but The Parkinson's club.

Route 63 is about travelling around England with Parkinson's and a free bus pass (I haven't managed to wangle one of those yet). It isn't entirely about the condition, but it does crop up as a recurring theme. As Dave so wisely remarks: 'Parkinsons enables you to make a bad impression much more cheaply than before.'

Members of the Parkinson's club progressively lose pieces of themselves. We forget how to walk. Our arm muscles get weaker. Our movements slow down. Our hands fumble doing simple tasks like buttoning a shirt or balancing food on a fork. Our faces no longer express emotions. Our

Foreword

voices lose volume and clarity. Our minds, in time, may lose their sharpness and more much more.

Thankfully, as this brilliant book proves, Dave has lost none of his sharpness, dry wit and ability to tell a good old-fashioned tale.

From the Rick Stein 'bargain' meal that cost the same as a chip shop in Hull to a man making a grand entrance on a bear, this book skilfully intertwines a trip on one hundred buses with thoroughly entertaining historical and sporting references, all of it cleverly woven together with the odd glass of real ale thrown in along the way.

Dave Hadfield proves that a diagnosis of an incurable illness isn't the end, but that it can be the start of a great adventure. Sometimes on a shiny red bus.

Dave Clark,
June 2015

Revving Up

🚌

BUS – it's a strangely unsatisfactory word, especially if you adopt the officially approved Northern pronunciation of 'buzz.' If it doesn't look or sound quite right in either version, that's because it's the tail-end of another word – omnibus. In three years of compulsory Latin, they never told me anything remotely as interesting as how the word the Romans used to mean 'for everyone' came to denote one of the cumbersome vehicles parked in front of the school whilst we waited for our liberation from our *amo, amas, amat*.

It's the French who are primarily responsible. An entrepreneur in the city of Nantes started to run a novel horse-drawn wagonette service in the 1820s. It was cheap and cheerful, and therefore for everyone. The x-factor that made the name stick was that there was a hatter's shop across the street from the terminus called Omnes. That had a certain ring to it – Omnes' Omnibus – but, by the time there were similar services in Paris and London, the Omnes was dropped, followed eventually by the Omni and by the horse, as it was replaced by steam and diesel. You can read a Shakespeare Omnibus, listen to *The Archers* Omnibus, or watch the *Coronation Street* Omnibus. The only context, however, in which the word omnibus is still commonly used for what we now call a bus, plain and simple, is in The Man on the Clapham Omnibus. This mythical citizen was the invention of the 19th century courtroom. He was used as a shorthand for the typical, reasonable man and what he could be expected to think. Clapham, at the time, was regarded as a sufficiently nondescript suburb for someone on his way there to be cast in the role of Mr Average; an Everyman in the vehicle for Everyone.

There are equivalent phrases in Melbourne and Sydney; the Man on the Bourke Street Tram and The Man on the Bondi Tram respectively. In Hong Kong, there is The Man on the Shaukiwan Tram. By a preposterous coincidence, I have been two of these Men, or as near as damn it. I travelled to work in Sydney on the successor to the Bondi Tram, which is now the Bondi suburban rail-line, followed by the Bondi bus; not to be confused with the Bendy-bus, which comes around the corner a little later. In Hong Kong, the rickety double-decker trams that still form the backbone of the city's street transport system went right past my door on their way to Shaukiwan. As for Bourke Street, I fear that I may have missed my chance, but I see nothing that should prevent me from being The Man on the Clapham Omnibus, however briefly. Surprisingly, America does not seem to have a similarly representative passenger. The Man on the Greyhound Bus, perhaps, if the Greyhound was a bus, which it isn't.

The closest it comes is the rhetorical question: 'How will it play in Peoria?' The small city in Illinois is supposed to be so average that hitting the right button there is as good as getting it right in 50 states. The Man on the Peoria Ommibus, however, is strangely silent.

Of course, the bus isn't really for everyone. I know people who haven't been on one for decades and would have to be dragged, kicking and screaming, anywhere near one. George Harrison used to insist that his attitude was a model of consistency. He hated the dirty, smelly things when he had to travel on them; later on, he hated them because they got in the way of his big, flash car. And his dad was a bus-driver.

Then there's the slur, often attributed to Mrs Thatcher, to the effect that any man travelling by bus after the age of 30 – or was it 35? It makes no odds to me – is, by definition, a failure. It's true that some motorists achieve an almost phallic satisfaction from sitting in their stationary vehicles during rush hour; but, to paraphrase a wiser man than me, have you seen the length of the 8.15 from Horwich Parkway to Manchester Piccadilly? And the 501 to Farnworth isn't bad either. I don't know where the Bendy-bus fits into this line of thinking. It is a particular bête noire of car drivers, however, probably because of its ability to block two streets simultaneously, the one you're on and the one at right-angles to it.

I don't remember there being buses in the first two towns in which I lived, but my dad remembers them coming to Hayfield. When he was a little lad in the 1920s, his home village's only links with the rest of Derbyshire and the world beyond were the train to New Mills and the car in which the local butcher, Bagshaw Beaver – I kid you not – would sometimes ferry people around. When he earned a scholarship to the secondary school, they issued him with a train pass. Then they introduced a bus service and paid him an equivalent subsidy, but he often used to walk to save the money. 'Well, tuppence ha'penny was tuppence ha'penny,' he says.

Route 63

I went to school when we lived in West London on a home-made seat on the back of his converted woman's pedal-bike, which sounds terrifying, but I do remember there being buses. One went past our flat above the bakers' shop with the destination 'Harrow on the Hill' up front and that always seemed vaguely exotic. There was another that went to Ruislip Lido, a flooded gravel pit where Londoners used to go for a wallow in hot weather. Walk to the junction with the main road and there were trolley buses to Uxbridge. You can almost taste the excitement.

Growing up in Bolton, it was two buses to school; the 1, 3 or 5 into town, then the 45 up Tonge Moor Road. If you wanted to go further afield, say to Manchester or Leigh, you had to get a bus of a different colour, with a different number, from a different stop, as like as not manned by a driver (and, in those days, a conductor too) speaking a subtly different language. Buses in Leigh, for instance, were lower than the rest, with four seats alongside each other upstairs, rather than pairs separated by a gap. The access was by a slightly sunken aisle, which reduced the height of the roof and enabled the bus to get under Leigh's low bridges. That had the additional advantage of allowing miners who had just finished their shift to lie full-length across the four seats, which they happily did. Warning: This might well be the only reference in this book to matters like the configuration of seats. As for what goes on under the bonnet, there could and should be no mention at all. I'm simply not interested; on the other hand, I'm very interested in where buses go and who goes on them.

At this stage, then, a definition. What is the difference between a bus and a coach? For the purposes of these travels, a bus is any vehicle where you can pay your fare on board. That means that Greyhound Buses, in America or Australia, are coaches, as is the Magic Bus in Britain. On the other hand,

Dustin Hoffman and Katharine Ross make their getaway at the end of *The Graduate* on a bus. The Civil Rights battle over who sat where was fought out on the back seats of buses. A bus generally has a nutter on board; you have to book one in advance if you want to be sure of one on a coach.

The really crucial difference is that, since 2006, buses have been free. If you're over pension age or have the greater good fortune to be disabled, you can travel all over England for nowt, nothing, nada. That means that, provided time is no object, you can travel from Berwick-upon-Tweed to Lands End buckshee, simply by flashing your bus pass at a succession of grumpy drivers. Well, I say grumpy; they are round here, unless, that is, I get one of the bold, brave lads I used to play rugby league with. Then they can't do enough for you, including leaving other passengers standing at bus-stops in order to get me back in time for last orders, or, on one occasion, going miles off route to drop me off at the end of my street. Try getting Virgin Rail to do that.

Another outstanding example of co-operation was the driver who used to bring me and my editor, Denis Mann, back from our jobs in Blackburn. He could be persuaded to get his clog down and arrive in the village of Tockholes several minutes early. That gave us time to nip into the Royal Arms for a couple of very swift pints while he puffed contentedly on his pipe outside in his cab.

There's another aspect of bus travel that I've found surprisingly user-friendly. Since I acquired this tremor from my Parkinson's disease, the most soothing place to be can be on a rumbling double-decker. It must be something to do with one lot of vibrations cancelling out another. Apart from that, there aren't a lot of advantages in carrying a disabled pass, rather than a plain, ordinary pensioners' one. You don't get to pull rank and order people out of the priority seats.

Be that as it may, free travel is hugely popular amongst both categories of user. Anything free is hugely popular, in fact, amongst the elderly and, now that I'm one of them – albeit on a slightly different pass – I'm all for it too. The trouble is that the scheme allegedly costs £1.1 billion a year and there have been grumblings from various think-tanks that it should be scrapped, or at least restricted.

Don't even think about it. For one thing, the maths are dodgy, because they include journeys that would not otherwise take place on buses that would be running anyway. It's impossibly complicated, but the general thrust is that no company should be better off or worse off as a result of carrying pass-holders. For another thing, the reaction to any tinkering with this pensioners' perk would make the Poll Tax Riots look like a Young Conservatives garden party. Trafalgar Square will be seething with angry old burghers – it will be like *Last of the Summer Wine* meets *Les Misérables* – and they will all have got there by bus, for free, or by train, for a 30 per cent reduction. For that, you need a Senior Railcard.

I gave my last one so much hammer that the print wore off it, so that the station staff became dubious about accepting it. Fortunately, one of them knew what to do. He got out his fag-lighter and applied the flame to the card, whilst I looked on like a volunteer having his watch smashed by a conjuror. Just before the pass was ready to burst into flames, he removed it from the heat and, as if by magic, the expiry date stood out clearly against the charred background.

I haven't asked him where he learnt this trick, but it looks a bit like the French Resistance or the adventures of the Secret Seven. Needless to say, I hope, do not try this with a Concessionary Bus Pass, as it is made of plastic and will melt. With that, I conclude the practical advice I have to offer.

HEADING
SOUTH

Greater Manchester - a state of mind

WHEN I decided upon this little jaunt, it was because it was an adventure I could have without needing a body that works properly any more. Other people might be carrying me around in their vehicles, rather than me travelling under my own steam, but it's still an adventure, because there are so many things that can go wrong.

I wanted to plan it, but to leave scope for going off at a tangent, if that was the way it worked out. My first port of call, therefore, was a transport bookshop near Piccadilly Station in Manchester, in search of some sort of master timetable, or at least an atlas of bus routes. You would have thought I'd asked for something so disgusting and disturbing that it couldn't be kept on even the loftiest of top shelves; some hard-core travel porn. 'No, we've got nothing like that,' said the trembling sales assistant. 'It's the bus companies, you see. They won't talk to each other.'

Next stop was my friend Andrew, who used to be a bus route planner, no less. He steered me towards various county council websites, most, if not all of which carry details of services within their boundaries. I started to put together an itinerary that would, very approximately, take me south to Lands End, east to Dover, north to Newcastle and back home to Bolton. How hard could that be? Three or four weeks away from hearth and home. A lot of sitting around, but first a certain amount of preparation.

I've never needed much persuading to travel light, but for this sort of jaunt, it is essential. Buses aren't designed to carry luggage any bulkier than a couple of bags of shopping, so you shouldn't really take anything that you can't balance on your knee. A small backpack, the sort I normally carry my lap-top around in, should be just about right. As for the contents, I made a list, ripped it up, made another, ripped that up and settled for the third. Allowing for a few crossings-out, it read like this:

4 shirts, 5 pants, shorts, pills (when you take as many as I do, they are best arranged in a sort of compartmentalised - with the emphasis on the 'mental' - tray, which can double up as a rather interesting percussion instrument if I stumble upon a jam session), toiletries (toothbrush and paste, talc, mouthwash, deodorant - don't want to make anyone else's journey a misery, do we?); mobile phone; iPod and respective chargers. Plastic file for cuttings, timetables etc. Small format British atlas (99p from all cheap book shops), water and snacks, bus pass (should be obvious, but you'd be surprised how often we old fogeys forget it. I still draw the line at wearing it round my neck on a lanyard).

Now, eagle-eyed readers will have spotted a controversial omission from this kit-list – socks. This is the result of a policy decision. Getting the damn things on and off must now take at least an hour a week; it's time you can't afford when you've got a bus to catch. I'll still wear them for weddings, funerals, cup finals and the like, but, after extensive trials, I've come to the conclusion that they serve no useful purpose. Provided your feet can breathe in your shoes – leather lined with Gortex are best, although the Lapps swear by a handful of grass in each – they will be dry and comfortable without socks. It cuts down on laundry, of course, although you will still need to seek out a launderette from time to time – and they are nothing like as numerous as they used to be, especially in the vicinity of bus stations. There's always the guest-house wash-basin, of course, but every time you use it for this you will rejoice that you don't have to wash your socks as well.

So, we're all packed and ready to go; the question is where to start. In my case, it's easy; out of the front door, turn left, down to the end of the street, left again and there's the stop for the 501.

We go back a long way, the 501 and me. The other end of the route, then the simple but prestigious number 1, used to link me with the town centre. I never knew where it went after that; I do now, because it goes through town and finishes near my present abode. It's the best bus in Bolton, because it also runs through the hospital grounds, so, no matter how grim times get, how deep the cutbacks, it can't be scrapped nor its frequency greatly reduced, unless people stop getting sick.

It has also been known to bring out the caring, sharing side of its drivers. Not long after I completed the travel for this book, I was on the 501 when a fellow-passenger I knew by sight got on, sat down and appeared to have some sort of seizure. After that, he slumped motionless in his seat and seemed as though, like an out-of-date day ranger ticket, he might have expired.

'He's just pissed,' said the driver. 'He's always riding around on here like that.'

Several of us tried to revive him and were convinced that there was something seriously wrong.

'Well, we're going to the hospital now and if he still hasn't moved I'll drop him off there.'

His diagnosis must have been broadly correct for I saw the comatose man a few weeks later, fit and well and hurrying to catch a bus. He was luckier than Mr George Ainsworth, an 84-year-old knocked down and killed by a 501 in November 2014. Whilst researching that unfortunate event, I wandered into a blog entirely devoted to journeys on the 501 route in Sydney (Town Hall to West Ryde). That was my bus on one of my sojourns in that fair city. Weird or what?

Then there was a puzzling incident on the 501 on my way to my dad's house. Out of the blue a disembodied voice declared: 'This bus is under attack. Please phone 999.' All the passengers laughed nervously, because we live in times where it is just about conceivable that the 501 bus might come under attack, be it from the brick-chuckers of New Bury or from a more shadowy and sinister organisation. I quizzed the driver as I got off and he showed me the alarm button he had inadvertently pressed with his right knee, thus triggering World War III.

Not just a transport link, the 501 you see, but the fourth emergency service, a portal to all the world's knowledge and a potential global flashpoint. And there's one due at 9.32. Like comedy, free bus travel is a matter of – wait for it – timing. Monday to Friday, it only kicks in at 9.30, so that we will not impinge on commuters. Try rolling up at 9.29

and some miserable driver will bar your way as though his life depends upon it. The only silver lining is that, if you keep the argument going long enough, it ticks around to half past and you win anyway. The same tactic doesn't work at midnight, when buses and their passes turn into pumpkins. Old freeloaders aren't really meant to be out at that time.

Anyway, there's no doubt about my legitimacy the morning I set out for a trial run. It's 9.43 before three buses turn up together in formation, their drivers having enjoyed their first leisurely and convivial brandies and cigars of the day at the turn-around up the road. My mate, the bus route planner, tells me that this is a phenomenon called bunching and that there is a mathematical model to explain why it happens, rather than merely being a case of drivers preferring safety in numbers. Be that as it may, it has a knock-on effect on the whole day, culminating in me being in Nantwich rather than Whitchurch. But that's much later, in a land far, far away (Cheshire); first we must tackle the abomination that is Greater Manchester.

I know nobody likes what any boundary commission does to their county. I still get poison-pen letters from Hull every time I mention Humberside, even when it is clear that I mean it merely as 'place by the side of the Humber,' rather than a widely unloved and now abolished unit of local government. The story of Greater Manchester is even messier. Edward Heath made it out of bits of Lancashire and Cheshire – and a couple of shavings of Yorkshire – whilst handing over other lumps to Merseyside, and it is the botched job you would expect of him. Somewhere like Bolton is in Greater Manchester for some purposes and still in Lancashire for others. Greater Manchester Council is defunct, but all maps – even 99p ones – dutifully delineate its boundaries. I know nobody who has ever written it in an address, even in order to send a threatening letter.

Route 63

Before the inception of Greater Manchester, the bus providers had a trial run with something called SELNEC. The ugliest acronym in the world, it stood for South East Lancashire North East Cheshire. They had a far-flung empire called the Trans-Lancs Express, which trundled all the way from Wigan, through Leigh to Oldham, Rochdale and even Stockport. It had all the hard-core bus enthusiasts at school very excited indeed. The real education for me, though, was the 82 from Bolton to Leigh. There was constant tension and hostility on that route because of Leythers' complaints that the seats that were rightfully theirs were being taken by people from Daubhill – Dobblers, as they were known – who had their own buses which they ought to have been on.

It was my first experience of bus route rage and I'll admit that I've seen worse since. There was that afternoon coming away from a match at Anfield when a gobby little Scouse scally was making a thorough nuisance of himself. When his mates got off halfway to town, a bunch of burly blokes blocked his exit and quietly but systematically duffed him up before letting him get off a couple of stops later, by now in tears and threatening to tell his mam.

Even that was mild compared with the time in Sumatra when our bus driver went through a roadblock. At the next checkpoint, he was stopped by furious soldiers, dragged off the bus and beaten with rifle-butts. When they thought he had learned his lesson, they let him get back behind the wheel and drive on, still bleeding, towards our destination. Even on the notoriously fractious 82, that didn't usually happen, even if you jumped a traffic light in Atherton. One connected public transport story, of sorts. At our destination in Sumatra, there was a boat service across the lake on market days. That sounded interesting and, according to the *Lonely Planet* guide that everyone carried, it cost only coppers. When we got on, the price had gone up – but only from 10 pence to 12 pence. It didn't seem too bad a case of inflation, but a pair of Scandinavian backpackers simply refused to pay the extra, because it said 10p in their guidebook. Possibly the ferry-men were trying it on, but what the hell. It became a complete impasse, with angry words exchanged in Swedish and Indonesian and a good deal of finger-pointing before the boatmen took command of the situation. They cut off the engines in the middle of the lake and both sides stubbornly rejected my offer to act as honest broker by paying the extra 2p myself.

We never got to the market. If we had, there would probably be another poorly-executed wood carving within arms-reach as I write this. It taught me something, though. You have to be flexible. The plan is to travel the length and breadth of England for nothing, but if it costs me 12 pence here and there, fair enough.

Bolton to Whitchurch

THE regular passengers on the 501 are a varied bunch. Among those I am never surprised to see are a bearded Asian woman, a permanently angry red-bearded, cursing Scotsman and two apparently unconnected chaps who are obviously former employees under the misapprehension that they still work on the buses. They check passengers on and off and offer pieces of advice concerning route diversions and the like. They never work together and, if they happen to be on the same bus at the same time, they sit there glowering at each other, both embarrassed at finding an interloper getting in the way of them performing their duties.

Route 63

There is also what I can only describe as a bus groupie, a dumpy woman of indeterminate age who flirts outrageously with the male drivers. She sets out her stall beside the cab, directly below the sign that warns passengers not to speak to or otherwise distract the driver. I've always been curious about that 'otherwise distract' and what it might include, but, just in case she isn't distracting enough, she has a stealthy way of sticking her head into the driver's compartment, only withdrawing it reluctantly when she gets a stern look from one of the fantasy bus drivers. There is undeniably a certain glamour in travelling for a living, be it test pilots or long-distance lorry drivers, but the 501 bus, for heaven's sake. You don't expect to find it there.

None of these regulars are on board the day I set out on my first attempt, but my mate Bill is. He's well into his seventies, but has only recently become a frequent bus user. Until a couple of years ago, he was the sort of old-stager who used to walk everywhere. If our local cricket team was playing ten miles away, he would walk there, have a few pints and walk back. He was the sort of indestructible old bloke I aspired to become, like my 99-year-old dad. He catches the occasional bus now as well, but still seems to feel that he isn't quite entitled to be carried around for nothing.

No such qualms for me as I get to Bolton bus station and change onto the 582, successor to the notorious 82. Bolton and Leigh used to be linked by one of the world's first goods and later passenger railways, originally intended to carry raw cotton and coal to the mills. It is long since ripped up, with part of its route re-born as the Leigh bypass, and it is the 582 that connects the two towns. It goes through Daubhill, now a heavily Asian area, but with the occasional Polish food store among the odd fruit and vegetables from places East of Suez.

My school pal Terry lived around here when it was

still unreconstructed white working-class, but in some ways equally exotic. Terry and his family lived on pies and fish and chips from the chippy on the corner and fizzy drinks that were 90 per cent E numbers. His elder brother left his smouldering fag ends everywhere and they all farted when they felt like it. It was everything that life in a respectable, semi-detached home wasn't. From the top deck of the 582, you can just about see the factory gate against which we played football and cricket until after dark. Quite often, the gate won. I had to go several miles further along the route before I found something I could do slightly better. It happened that my new friends at school in Bolton were mainly from the Leigh, Atherton and Tyldesley direction. They therefore had different priorities, like rugby league and kicking Dobblers out of 'their' seats on the bus. They even had different names for the small towns where they lived: Leyth, Bent and Bongs. Westhoughton, on the other hand, was Cowyed City, because of an apocryphal story of a farmer who, when his cow got stuck in a gate, sawed off the unfortunate beast's head. His logic was that the gate cost more than the cow. Cowyeds are still regarded as being a bit like that; daft but crafty.

It wasn't quite like being brought up by wolves, but I was, in a manner of speaking, adopted by Leythers. I was a big, awkward kid, recently arrived from the soft and suspect South, but I had my uses on a rugby field. So I found myself, more and more often, staying on the 582 all the way to the terminus on Spinning Jenny Street to meet my Leigh cronies, for games and, not long after, for a few pints. They all drank mixed – half of mild split with a half of bitter – but I was used to the idea that things were slightly different once you got past Four Lane Ends. When I got on a 582 recently, there was a young lad in a bit of a panic. 'I'm meant to be going to somewhere called Dobble,' he said, 'but I can't find it anywhere. Only somewhere called Daub Hill.' Get on, son, you're in the right place.

The only other passenger on the top deck was another youngish man, who kept up a continuous running argument with himself in a sing-song language all his own. Naturally, he got off at Atherton, although I bet that, if he had let himself get a word in edgeways, he would have called it Bent. He could have been changing at the Bacca Shop for Bongs, who knows?

Atherton is a town for which the term 'unremarkable' is at least four syllables too long. It does have, however, the first remarkable pub on this book's route. The Pendle Witch is tucked away down an alley – you couldn't call it a street – and not only does it have the full range of Moorhouses beers, from faraway Burnley in East Lancashire, but also a number of dishes cooked, Belgian-style, in beer. It's tempting, but I've only been going for a few minutes and I've had my breakfast.

On the other side of Atherton, there is the well-preserved little industrial village of Howe Bridge, then the site of the old Lancashire United Transport bus garage and now an incongruous range of man-made green hills, moulded out of the slag heaps that used to stand here. Just short of Leigh town centre, set back a couple of streets on the right, used to be the Leigh rugby ground, Hilton Park. Like the shops and the traffic, though, that ground has been relocated out of town, on the mini-motorway that is Atherleigh Way. Nowadays, you can drive along this road and, in the space of a few hundred yards, pass Leigh's stadium and the grounds of the town's two leading amateur clubs, Leigh East and Leigh Miners Rangers. It's cosy, is what it is.

It's in the middle of the deeply depressed old town of Leigh, however, that you have to change onto one of two services to Warrington. There are advantages to being in Leigh; you can, for instance, struggle to pay more than £2 for a pint, although I doubt whether many people still know what constitutes a pint of mixed. The town also has its own signature dish – lobby, a sort of watery stew involving corned beef, or, as Wiganers say, a pie without the crust. I'd never thought of Leigh as much of a gastronomic melting pot – which sounds like the sort of cooking gimmick you might invest in when you'd exhausted the possibilities of the George Foreman Grill – so I was pulled up short when I saw this sign in the window of a pub near the Warrington bus stop: 'Special Today – Lobby Tikka Massala'. I've been trying ever since to imagine what it might be like, but possibly it's better left as that – one of the great imagined dishes of South Lancashire.

Yes, South Lancashire. That, if you ignore SELNEC and the GMC, is undeniably where we are. How come, then, that, a couple of miles out of town, we cross the East Lancashire Road? The clue lies in its Sunday name – the Liverpool and East Lancashire Road. The first custom-built inter-city highway in the country when it was opened by King George in 1934, it should have been the M62 of its day. The plan was that it would go right across Lancashire and right across Yorkshire as well to finish in Hull, but what with the war and a a couple of other distractions, it never got beyond Irlams o'th' Height, that notorious test of the correct use of the apostrophe, on the outskirts of Salford. You could hardly call it the Irlams o'th' Height Road, so the East Lancs stuck.

When you cross it coming from Leigh, you are immediately in a very different place; flat, fertile farmland planted with prosperous-looking villages – Glazebury, Culcheth, Croft. A string of attractive country pubs always seem reasonably busy. The best-named is the Comfortable

Gill at Glazebury; you can hardly imagine any trouble at throwing-out time at a pub called by that reassuring name. The gill – with a soft 'g' – is a Lancashire gill, which is half a pint, as opposed to the quarter-pint in the rest of the country. Maybe that is why they are so comfortable in Glazebury. Winwick, where the back-lanes meet the A49 and the motorway system, has a more disconcerting history, with the death of King Oswald of Northumbria, a battle in the Civil War, a rail crash in 1934 that killed 11 people and one of the biggest of the Victorian mental asylums on its conscience. The loony bin, as we children sensitively used to call it when we drove past, is now a posh housing estate, with gates to keep people out, rather than keep them in.

Warrington, a couple of miles over the M62, used to be the biggest brewing town in England – although Burton-upon-Trent might have disputed that – and part of the old Walker's Brewery site is now home to a thriving rugby league club. It's little wonder I have an affinity with the place. There is a problem, though. As well as a hold-up – caused by the traffic, rather than by a highwayman, I had better make clear at this point – coming out of Bolton and another one coming out of Leigh, they are digging up the A49 on the way into Warrington. It just isn't a very quick road. Chuck Berry used to get his kicks on Route 66; around here, you have to serve your time on the A49.

The upshot of it all is that I miss the connection with the bus for Northwich and, it being too early for a beer, I have the best part of an hour to kill in the bus station. Stretching a coffee and an Eccles cake as far as humanly possible, I reflect that there could be quite a lot of this sort of thing lying ahead of me, sitting in cafés waiting for buses. Once away from the town centre, over the Manchester Ship Canal and through Stockton Heath, we are soon in village Cheshire. In fact, we seem to go through most of the villages in Cheshire. Comberbatch has two pub names that are right up there with the Comfortable Gill. The Drum and Monkey is merely whimsical; the Spinner and Bergamot seems frankly undecipherable. It turns out to be named after two racehorses. The local landlord had one called The Spinner, after which he christened the pub. When an equally successful nag called Bergamot came along, it was tagged on as well. Anderton has England's only working boat-lift, connecting the River Weaver with the Trent and Mersey Canal, and Antrobus is worth going through just to be able to say that you've been on an omnibus in Antrobus.

I'm tempted to say that the South starts in Northwich; the salt certainly does. It's one of those towns with only one role in life, that being to deliver ton after ton of the white gold. Salt gets a bit of a bad press these days, as something largely to be avoided, so it is easy to forget what an essential commodity it has always been. It is rather a disappointment to find that it is twinned with Dole in France and Carlow in Ireland, rather than with somewhere with a similar connection to pepper. Chile, perhaps, well known for its red-hot peppers; perhaps not. A word of caution, though. In recent years, Northwich's salt has been extracted by a technique the sounds uncannily similar to fracking, flushing it out with high-powered jets of water, and the area is particularly susceptible to subsidence. There could be a warning in that.

There is just time to catch the bus to Crewe, passing through Winsford, a place that, when I mentioned my route to someone with some local knowledge, he damned with two of the most dismissive words in the English language – Scouse overspill. It does look like a slice of Scousopolis, transplanted to the Cheshire countryside. Scouse, by the way, is another species of crustless pie, distinguishable from lobby only by an expert. See, we aren't going anywhere near Liverpool and already you've learned all you need to know about the place.

As for Crewe, it's something of a rum set-up transport-wise. As a railway town, it's one of world's trailblazers. When the station was opened in 1837, it was to serve the village of Crewe, population 70, across the fields. As the station grew, so did the town surrounding it and it remains one of the busiest hubs in the country, nay the world. There are now 23 long-distance trains per hour running via its 12 bustling platforms, carrying over 2.3 million passengers a year. The train that was robbed in the Great Train Robbery came through Crewe and changed to a Crewe crew, including the driver, Jack Mills, who was so badly hurt in the much romanticised attack. Everything that is big in the world of trains has a Crewe connection. That might be why there was a sense of shock in the country when part of Crewe station's roof blew off in early 2014. Virgin Trains wheeled out a spokesperson with the curiously reassuring name of Sheila Breeze to tell the world that the station would soon be restored to its former glories.

Crewe bus station, on the other hand, is a couple of shelters around the back of Wetherspoons. If there was a battle between road and rail travel back in the day, Crewe seems to be conclusive evidence that rail won. Crewe also won the contest for significance with Nantwich, its older, posher and now much smaller neighbour. Like Winsford, it turned down the chance to have a main line station. To get to Whitchurch, however, you have to go through Nantwich.

'Yes, you do,' said the inspector on Crewe bus station. 'But I'm warning you now that I know ABSOLUTELY NOTHING about what goes on out there.'

Nantwich is all of four miles away, so it is to be expected that its customs and practices should be strange and incomprehensible. It's a slow four miles by bus, though, and by the time I get there I'm skewered by one of the traps that they hint at in Crewe. I arrive at 3.10 and the last bus for Whitchurch left at 3.05. Has nobody told them around here about the 24-hour society? Basically, I have a choice. I can turn right around and go home; after all, it is only a trial run. Or I can catch the train to Whitchurch and another train back. I opt for the latter, do a bit of reconnaissance in the town and depart with a heightened awareness of the sorts of things that can go wrong.

THERE are half a dozen Whitchurches in the UK; at least I didn't make the mistake of going to the wrong one. Two of the others are in Hampshire and South Wales, so it would be a time-consuming error.

I should remember the way to Whitchurch in Salop, however, on account of an unforgettable visit there in the mid-seventies. I was working for the *Shropshire Journal* series of weekly newspapers, based in Telford, but often sent out to the far-flung corners of the empire. Once I was so saturated after getting to Whitchurch on my motorbike that the only thing to do in the little one-man office in a parade of shops was to strip off and try to dry out my clothes in front of the electric fire whilst I clattered away on the typewriter. I could have sworn I'd locked the door behind me. The good news is that the lady with the results from the Women's Institute vegetable and produce show who proved that I hadn't is now out of therapy.

Route 63

If you take A. E. Housman as your guide to Shropshire, there is one respect in which you are bound to be disappointed. The most famous line he ever wrote concerns the county's 'blue remembered hills.' Blue, my foot. They are blue in the same way that the Blue Mountains in New South Wales are blue, or the Bluegrass country of Kentucky; that is, not blue at all. I can empathise with his desire to see blue where there is none. On family days out, we used to have a game of spotting the gaps in the generally leaden skies. The issue we would then discuss was whether there was enough blue to make a man a pair of trousers – blue jeans, no doubt. On a day when the sun seriously threatened to come out, there might be enough blue to make a whole suit of clothes; on a really grim day, only enough for a sock. It wasn't much of a game, but it made a change from I-Spy.

As for Housman, he coined one other phrase that everyone knows, if only because it became the title of a James Bond film – *Die Another Day*. I have searched his canon in vain for references to *Dr No* or *The Man With the Golden Gun*.

As a son of Worcestershire, he was writing not about his home county but about his melancholy love affair with the one on the far horizon, to an idealised version of which he felt drawn. To hook up with Housman, though, we have to get to the damn place ourselves and to do so requires a slight change of tactics. After jeopardising the entire project by briefly losing my wallet – pass, credit cards and all – on a bus (where else?) I finally achieved escape velocity.

One of the quirks of the Concessionary Bus Pass is that, at weekends, you can use it all day; provided there are any buses at all, of course, which, particularly on a Sunday, there quite frequently are not. Thus it is that on the Saturday of my 63rd birthday – no cards at this stage, please – I'm at the bus stop at the end of our street, waiting for the 501 due at 6.42. I'm through Bolton and Leigh whilst they both lie snoring and onto a 19 for Warrington that didn't even register when I planned the route on the internet.

This was lesson one: There's always a chance that there'll be a better connection than there's supposed to be and it's always worth checking out. It did mean a bit of rearranging with my bus route planner mate, Andrew. Whilst I was cruising through the village of Daresbury, home to Lewis Carroll and the scene of my best ever cricket innings – 69 not out for the *Bolton Evening News* on a dodgy track against the *Warrington Guardian* – he was rushing to get on the same, Chester-bound bus at a village called Mickle Trafford. Carroll, by the way, is the first marker on a thoroughly literary itinerary. Sadly, we will not be passing anywhere else notable for my cricketing successes.

The trouble with Mickle Trafford is that it is closed, or at least the road through it is, necessitating a diversion that takes the bus miles away. Fortunately, his old bus-routing instincts come to the fore and he parks up and climbs on board further towards Chester.

Chester is one of those places where the buses are – literally – all over the shop. It's not the first thing they tell you in the guidebooks, but it's true. It involves a slog through the tourist hordes to the Whitchurch stop. Plan A was to overnight in Whitchurch, but when I started making phone calls, the place appeared to be full. 'There must be a wedding on or something,' said the third and last place I tried. Plan B was to carry on to Shrewsbury and Ludlow. At least, I assured Andrew, there would be no complications in Salop; simply arrive at the bus station on one bus and leave on another.

For my first two jobs in journalism – in Oswestry to the north and Telford to the east – Shrewsbury had been the big town to go to at weekends, but I had always thought of it as rather a sedate place. Mind you, years later when I called in at the office of the *Shrewsbury Chronicle* to see an old colleague, I was told that he was in hospital after being set alight – presumably by a disgruntled reader. In most parts of the country, they write a letter to the editor.

Shrewsbury was also home to one of my favourite English eccentrics – 'Mad Jack' Mytton. Actually, eccentric doesn't quite cover it. His relatively short life – he died of sheer wear and tear at the age of 38 – was described as 'a series of suicide attempts.' Here are just a few examples to give you the general flavour. He once arrived at a banquet riding a bear, he set fire to his nightshirt to cure the hiccups and he took 2,000 bottles of port with him to Cambridge to sustain him through his studies. He was also Tory MP for Shrewsbury, although that seems almost incidental.

He is not the only local celebrity, of course, not with Charles Darwin to contend with, whilst from Wem, the only substantial town between Whitchurch and Shrewsbury, we have the bloody legacy of George Jeffreys, better known as Hanging Judge Jeffreys, the man sent to the West Country to prosecute and dispatch those implicated in the Monmouth Rebellion.

There are historians now who claim that Jeffreys was no better nor worse than the norm at the time and that he got his bad name because he was often drunk and irascible in court. All the same, if I'd been appearing before him, I think I'd pull the old magistrates' court scam of asking for an adjournment and waiting for the Wrist Slapping Judge or the Community Service Judge.

It is hard to avoid the River Severn in Shrewsbury, looping around the town centre as it does, almost turning it into an island. No wonder it is a flood hotspot. It is one of those English towns that exact a tax from the people wealthy enough to live in its nicest houses – the ones by the river – in the form of regular bailing out. Even more vulnerable are homes and businesses actually on the river. I used to be particularly fond of a floating Thai restaurant, but one year, after unusually heavy rain, I went to its mooring and found... nothing. There was a chap of vaguely oriental appearance, so I asked him where it was. 'Bewdley,' he said. 'Float away.'

The local football club, Shrewsbury Town – where the England goalkeeper, Joe Hart, among others, learned his trade – got around the problem of excessive proximity to England's most potentially destructive river by having a man in a coracle to retrieve balls from the Severn. That was when they were at their historic home, Gay Meadow; now, like so many other clubs in all sports, they are miles out of town.

So am I when the bus makes its surprising final stop. I had completely disregarded Shrewsbury Carnival. The procession of floats filled the town centre and blocked off all the routes to the south. You couldn't go around it, you couldn't go through it; the stewards saw to that. Somewhere beyond it, but unreachable, was the bus for Ludlow. What you could just about get away with doing was joining the parade in that general direction, trying to look like you belonged and occasionally waving to the crowd. We must have looked like beaten finalists in the Over-60s backpack-carrying event and drew a smattering of sympathetic applause at a couple of points on the route.

It did the job, though; it got me on the bus to Ludlow and Andrew, eventually, back to his parked-up support vehicle in Whitchurch. It was also, along with the Mickle Trafford business, a timely illustration of Lesson Two: Expect the Unexpected.

You are soon out of Shrewsbury and into the countryside that Housman celebrated in 'A Shropshire Lad.'

'Into my heart an air that kills
From yon far country blows:
What are those blue remembered hills,
What spires, what farms are those?

That is the land of lost content,
I see it shining plain,
The happy highways where I went
And cannot go again.'

I remember them as happy highways, if rather lengthy and occasionally tricky ones, in the scorching summers of 1976 and 1977, when I covered a patch stretching from Staffordshire to Aberystwyth on a 125cc motorbike – the most powerful you could ride without taking the test I would most assuredly have failed. As it was, I left a fair bit of leather on country lanes when I misjudged bends. It is in marginally more comfort and safety than that in which we drift south on the A49 through places like Church Stretton and Craven Arms, where I used to cover the meetings of the town councils. The road is at its best when it squeezes between the Long Mynd on the right and Wenlock Edge on the left. And yes, there is a tinge of blue about them, if I remember rightly.

The town that ate itself

I CAN never approach Ludlow without a shiver of guilt and humiliation. It was there in that early spring of what became a career that I was paraded in shame before the assembly of an entire primary school after writing an April Fool story in the *South Shropshire Journal*, claiming that Ludlow Castle had been bought by Americans and was going to be exported, stone by stone.

It was like one of those public criticism sessions during the Cultural Revolution. I had to stand there, head bowed, with about 120 solemn little faces looking at me reproachfully, admit that it had been very silly to make up such a story and agree with the headmaster that there was nothing clever about worrying the children like that.

Only marginally less intimidating is the reputation that Ludlow has built up since then as the most wonderful place on God's earth. John Betjeman called it 'the pleasantest town in England' and that was before it embraced the concept of the 'slow' town, which he surely would have applauded. This slow town business, though, it's alright if you're not in a hurry. For instance, someone might start pulling you a pint of Ludlow Gold, but break off in the middle to have a chat about metaphysics. It's fine if you're not thirsty.

What Ludlow is really famous for, though, is feeding its face with fabulous food, in its capacity as the unofficial Foodie Capital of England. This is a town with restaurants with national and international reputations and a magnificent food market. Even the burger van has a Michelin star and every packet of pork scratchings has its provenance documented. There must be people in Ludlow who live on baked beans, straight from the can, but you don't come across them. It has its own sauce, made from spring onions and Shropshire Blue cheese, that can make just about anything taste good. Ah yes, the blue remembered cheese; maybe that's what Housman was thinking of.

I'm lucky to have a room amid this cornucopia. In fact, I've been double-booked at my bed and breakfast and traded off, like an unwanted prop forward nearing the end of his career, to an establishment a little further up Gravel Hill. My original digs could hardly have been any more comfortable than the ones to which I was transferred; when I was shown to my room I felt like I was making it untidy just by standing there.

And then, the inevitable question in Ludlow: Where to eat. I'm slightly constrained because I'm contractually obliged to be in front of a TV in a public place for England's World Cup match at 11 pm, in order to write about it for *The Independent*. That rules out seven courses of fine dining and induces a rather bloody-minded counter-strategy. Surely, the challenge in Ludlow is not to eat well, but to eat badly and write scathingly about it; it must be possible. After a quick tour of the town centre – the Buttermarket Cross, the improbably ornate half-timbering of The Feathers, the Castle (still intact) – I settle on a place that seems to have set itself an impossible task. The courtyard looks inviting in the evening sunlight, but 'Thai Tapas,' what on earth can that be? Two entirely different cultures and cuisines; it must be a recipe not so much for fusion food as for confusion food. But, wouldn't you know it in Ludlow, it works; washed down with a pint of Hobson's Best Bitter – from Cleobury Mortimer, about seven miles away, it all makes perfect sense.

I think I'm onto a winner when I get a bit peckish whilst watching the latter stages of that ill-fated match in the early hours of the morning. The pub where I'm ensconced has a sort of snack bar attached. There, in the pie-warmer is one last, lonely pasty. Surely this must be the back-to-basics experience which I crave. But no, it's infuriatingly delicious. It tastes like fillet steak in a red wine jus, with shallots and just a hint of anchovy, all wrapped in delicate pastry that melts in the mouth. Damn!

Some people I spoke to predicted trouble from the

town's small, select band of resident yobs after the match. As I walked back to my digs, however, all that could be heard was the occasional discreet pop of wine corks and the murmur of civilised conversation.

Suddenly, though, there parked around a corner was an ambulance, a vehicle that seemed to hint at disorderly behaviour; a little like the paddy wagons that park just off the main square in Pontefract on Friday and Saturday nights, when scrapping is mandatory. Clearly, something of the sort was expected in Ludlow, albeit on a smaller scale. As I drew close, I saw the inscription: 'Emergency Poet.'

I think old Betjeman would have found that perfectly pleasant, but there was a faint churning sound from the direction of St Lawrence's Church, where A. E. was turning in his grave at such levity about poetry in his adopted county.

I wonder too what either of them would have made of something else I saw in Ludlow. As I walked down towards the Ludford Bridge over the River Teme, there was a downward flash of white.

'Did you see that?' asked a chap who was looking down onto the water. 'Seagull took a duckling. Killed all the cygnets last year as well. Never used to happen. Never saw a seagull here 'til three years ago.'

The duck and her surviving young were swimming around in distraught circles and you could understand their disorientation. After all, you can't get much further from the sea in this country than Ludlow. The gulls should have been living comfortably on discarded fast food in Aberystwyth or Weston-super-Mare, not dive-bombing the River Teme. There would be plenty of vulnerable young waterfowl on the coast as well. Then the truth struck me; yes, even the live ducklings, with their perfect balance between the fluffy and the crunchy, taste better in Ludlow.

And one last message for anyone who was traumatised by the front page of the *South Shropshire Journal* 40 years ago. I understand that the Yanks have come back with an improved offer for the castle.

IT was a predictably excellent breakfast, with just about everything rigorously sourced from local suppliers. Bacon from this butcher, sausages from that farm, baked beans from Heinz, free range eggs. Everything you could wish to know, apart from the names of the pig and the hen.

Outside the Assembly Rooms, the bus for Hereford is late and the driver looks like he has had a good breakfast. Not that it matters; on a Sunday, you can get to Hereford, or out to my personal favourite Shropshire town, Bishops Castle, but not much further. In fact, my research department has found out in the nick of time that, a year later, the Sunday service to Hereford has been withdrawn; a reminder of the tenuous nature of many local transport links. I'm on the first of the three available buses on summer Sundays in 2014, however, out over the Teme, with no ducklings in evidence. In Richards Castle, on the Shropshire-Herefordshire border, I spot a signpost that stirs my pride in English place names.

I've heard it said that it's only American towns and cities that have the music in them. 'Route 66' is famous enough to have its title filched and adapted by this volume. Mainly associated with Chuck Berry, it was in fact written by one Bobby Troup and recorded by everyone from Nat King Cole to the Rolling Stones. And the itinerary it reels off has an undeniable resonance, especially as it gets further from Chicago and closer to LA: Amarillo, Gallup, Flagstaff, Barstow, San Bernardino.

As an alternative invitation to spend your time on the A49, we have Wigan, Warrington, Whitchurch, Shrewsbury, Ludlow – don't forget Leominster – Hereford and Ross on Wye. It has a music of its own; a march for the Marches, perhaps. Billy Bragg celebrated the A13 through Essex and, for sheer quantity of obscure place names, there is Flanders and Swann's 'The Slow Trains.' Here on a wonky fingerpost in Richards Castle, though, is a pointer to a place I must visit one day; welcome to Goggin – and, a few seconds later, we're past the turning and wondering whether such a place could really exist. My 1952 *Ordnance Survey* map of the area shows Goggin – or, strictly speaking, The Goggin – as a few black dots about half a mile away; more of a hamlet than a village, but it went straight to the pinnacle of my Top Ten English Place Names.

Between Leigh and Warrington, on certain bus routes, you go through the sinister settlement of Locking Stumps, which sounds like a spell cast by a particularly malign local coven of witches. A mate of mine got a teaching job there and, needless to say, was never heard of again.

I'd passed another candidate the following day – No Man's Heath, near Malpas in Cheshire. It is one of two villages of that bleak and draughty name; the other is in Warwickshire. There is also a No Man's Land in Cornwall, whilst I will never be able to listen to two people nattering on pointlessly without being transported to those garrulous neighbours in Sussex, East and West Wittering. I can't believe that I won't be able to offer you some similar delights as we wend our way onwards.

One added benefit on this bus was a chap in a Spurs

shirt who was delivering a seminar on exactly why England had lost to Italy the previous night to a fellow traveller. When his original audience got off in Leominster – a pleasant enough place, but not worth the three hours I would have had to spend there – and a new passenger got on, I thought 'Here we go again.' But not a bit of it. He delivered an equally impassioned and well worked-out lecture, but came to diametrically opposite conclusions. If he's not a local councillor, he should be.

Meanwhile, across the aisle, two enormously fat girls are describing, in alarming detail, what they are going to do if they ever get their hands on some unfortunate young lad, who apparently fancies them both rotten.

We go into Hereford past United's rusty old ground on Edgar Street, scene of arguably the most famous FA Cup goal of all time when Ronnie Radford hacked one out of the mud and into the back of the Newcastle net from 30 yards in 1972. Not much glory these days, with the club facing possible closure and hoping for reinstatement somewhere even further down the league ladder.

FIRST priority in Hereford is to get to the cathedral and see the world's largest chained library. They must have had real problems with stolen and overdue books in Hereford, because the second-biggest chained library is here too, as well as the remarkable *Mappa Mundi*, the first recognisable map of the world, thought to have been created around 1300 – or two hours before I arrived.

The trouble is that at 3.00pm on a Sunday, the part of the cathedral that houses it is closed for a service. Not to worry, there's a facsimile accessible; better still, its colours make it much more like the original when it was freshly painted, so that will do me just fine. It's a mighty piece of work, the size of a large cow, because that, essentially, is what it's painted on. For theological reasons, Jerusalem is the centre of the world and the British Isles are crammed down in a corner. No bus routes and no trace of a hamlet called The Goggin.

Any right-thinking person likes a good map, I think. I had planned to take quite a few with me on this trip, especially since I found a second-hand bookshop in Horwich that sells the handsome 1952 *Ordnance Survey* series at a quid a throw. You can buy one to study over a pint at dinner time. Put a few of them together, though, and they weigh surprisingly heavy, so I had to make some weighty decisions. In the end, I whittled it down to the two turning points of the journey, Lands End and East Kent, in the modern series, and left the rest at home. The contemporary maps are a useful aid to navigation; the 1952 ones are a work of art and a thing of beauty.

The same could not be said, as I approached it on the lorry-laden Hereford ring-road, of the bed and breakfast in which I had booked. With its dirty, neglected façade and a few broken windows, it looked as though, in season, it would have held around 35 East European fruit-pickers. And, out of season, no-one at all. There was a handwritten note pinned to the door, giving a mobile number to ring if you arrived before 8.00pm. I'd already decided I wasn't staying there. I walked towards the bus station and found a pub with accommodation. It was rather more than I wanted to pay and the landlady seemed a bit of a dragon, but it had to be the better option. You don't want to lower the whole tone of the expedition by staying in a doss-house. My mum, with her serial rejection of hotel rooms as not up to her standards, would for once have been proud of me.

On St Owen Street nearby, there was a pub I wanted to try, the first, despite what people might say about this being a glorified pub crawl, that was new to me.

Barrels is the brewery tap for the Wye Valley brewery, serves their full range of beers and, apart from a really lousy name, is everything you would want from a county town pub on a flawless summer Sunday. The garden is full and animated, the rooms around the bar shady and quiet.

In their main square, most large towns or small cities have a statue of an eminent citizen; in Hereford's case, Nell Gwynn perhaps, or Gilbert Harding or Beryl Reid. Or, if you really wanted to make a statement, the entire original line-up of Mott the Hoople.

Not in this square; it is dominated by a life-sized Hereford bull. Maybe I'm easily impressed, but this particular example of the breed seems to add extra weight to the expression 'well-hung beef.' I understand that there are militant prudes in the world, who have been known to take a mallet and chisel to the crown jewels of statues, animal or human. If they were to try that sort of thing in Hereford, they would need a chainsaw and possibly a small charge of dynamite.

The surprising thing, in a city so proud of its beef, is that none of the pubs and restaurants around the square makes a big thing about its availability. No Hereford steak burgers that I could find. But then all the prime cuts had probably been sent to Ludlow.

Hereford to Gloucester

UP bright and early for another powerhouse breakfast. Wasn't it Hilaire Belloc who said that the only meal the English could make properly was breakfast and that the visitor was probably best to order that three times a day?

The service for Gloucester is at the bus station right across the street. You have to be careful to get the right one, because we're flirting with Wales here. You can't, for instance, change buses at Monmouth, because that takes you across the border, where your free pass is no longer valid and the bus turns into a pumpkin and the driver into Hanging Judge Jeffries – to take in vain the name of the North Shropshire town of Wem's most famous citizen.

No such problems with going through Ross on Wye, although, like all the towns in the Marches, it has a distinctly Welsh flavour. It was in Hereford that I heard an elderly couple assert their national identity.

'This World Cup thing,' says she. 'Are we in it?'

'Don't know,' says he. 'Don't think so.'

The route to Ross is largely off the main roads; within a few miles, we go through or past Little Birch, Much Birch, Little Dewchurch and Hoarwithy, to name only the most evocative villages, and it's as picturesque as it sounds. The day being as clear as a bell, you can make out the Black Mountains on the right and the Malverns on the left. The bus stops in Ross are on Cantilupe Street, which is a hard location to forget. It seems that Ross must be the only town in the country with a bus station named after a melon. In fact, it refers to Thomas de Cantilupe, a 13th century Bishop of Hereford and saint in the making.

The highlights of the road to Gloucester are the villages of Boxbush and Solomon's Tump, both just over the county boundary.

Like Herefordshire, Gloucestershire has more than its share of spectacular place names. Nowhere matches Hereford, though, for its really useful crops, seen for miles through the bus window – hops and, if you like that sort of thing – cider apples. The whole county is a booze-up waiting to happen, but it would have been a poor one without the introduction of hops from France, converting the original English beverage of ale into what we now call beer.

No time to slake the thirst that these musings inevitably induce. I have a bus to catch.

Diversion: Cirencester

CIRENCESTER isn't on my way. It isn't really on the way to anywhere. I want to go because, some time back in the mists of history, between Roman invasion and the invention of beer, I spent part of my childhood there.

That was where I started school, giving me a faint but annoying West Country twang that can still surface at times of high stress, chopping its way through the tangled undergrowth of a Lancashire accent like a rusty machete. On the map, it doesn't look as though it should be too difficult to get there from Gloucester, but at what is supposed to be its stand on the bus station its name is blanked out with sticky tape – never a good sign. I ask a couple of drivers.

'Cirencester?' says one with the air of a man unconvinced that there is any such place. 'I think we used to go there. We don't go there now.'

'Hang on,' says the other. 'Doesn't one of those purple buses go there? Just round the back and across the road.'

And there, sure enough, is the Pulhams service to Cirencester, just about to pull away. It's not exactly purple, more cream and maroon, but it'll do.

Pulhams, based at Bourton-on-the-Water and serving the north Cotswolds – south Cotswolds? Never heard of them – seem like a game little survivor of a small bus company, filling in a few of the gaps left by the bigger boys. The driver seems to know everybody who gets on and we cover a lot of miles collecting them. Spurning the A roads, the bus weaves through country lanes to a series of glowing stone villages. It is the last Monday on which it will do so as a matter of course. A notice on the bus says that, from the following week, the last bus from Gloucester – which, early in the afternoon, this one is – will no longer go via the villages unless requested to do so. A little bit of bus history in the making.

Cirencester itself is the most prosperous looking, poshest place on the entire route. A number of pubs have signs up saying 'No football. No TV.' The days when the town made a fortune from the Cotswold wool trade and built the cathedral-sized Church of St John the Baptist, the largest of all the 'wool' churches, do not feel all that distant. Looking a little further back, it claims to have been the second biggest Roman town in Britain, after London. I'm always sceptical of this sort of claim to fame. I bet there will be other contenders to that title further down the track. It was, however, almost certainly the biggest Roman settlement in the north Cotswolds.

What were we doing there? It was down to what seemed a tempting bakery job and a promotion for my dad. Unfortunately, it wasn't quite the job it appeared, because part of his role consisted of trying to extract the money owed by various stately homes and minor public schools. Such was the culture of entitlement in the Cotswolds in those days that none of these well-heeled customers thought they should pay. Trying to prise payment from them left its mark on my dad. Although deeply conservative in other respects, it gave him an abiding mistrust of 'toffs'. The other thing he remembers from our relatively short time there was trying to do anything with a back garden that consisted of a layer of clay on top of solid rock. He recalls planting his potatoes with the aid of a pickaxe.

Maybe he should also have used it on some of the bad payers, because within a couple of years the bakery had closed down and we were on the move again. I don't want to make it sound like *The Grapes of Wrath*, but it was a good early lesson in basic economics.

That was almost 60 years ago and I hadn't been back since. As I wait outside the Corn Hall on the Market Square for the bus back to Gloucester, however, I spot a few decayed old aristo types who look as though they haven't paid their bills at the bakers for a while, and give them a suspicious glare.

IT's the direct bus back to Gloucester, a place that never stops running itself down, via the brash self-confidence of Cheltenham. A mere four miles apart on the map, they are on different planets as far as their assessment of themselves and each other is concerned.

That is the reason for my chapter heading; not that I think Gloucester is such a terrible place, but that it rarely stops saying sorry for what it is and what it isn't.

'Don't know why you've come here,' they will tell you. 'Nothing much here.' Apart from the cathedral, of course, and a rugby union ground that would not feel out of place hosting league 200 miles north. A proper ground, that is, as opposed to a corporate back-scratching emporium like Harlequins, for instance.

They are heavily into their rugby union at the Linden Tree, the pub where I'm booked in for the night, but the major sport around the bar is running down Gloucester.

'My old dad, he used to say they're only interested in three things in Gloucester: beer, baccy and bingo. You can add another one now – benefits.' And that is from one of the comparatively pro-Gloucester voices. Even he argues that Gloucester gets nothing and Cheltenham gets everything. 'They got halfway through doing up the docks and they ran out of money,' he says.

In fact, Gloucester retains some of its maritime legacy. It has one of the longest-established black and Chinese populations in the country. The doorway next to the stop where I caught the bus to the Linden Tree advertised the offices of the Gloucester Chinese Women's Association – and they haven't got one of them in Cheltenham.

What they have, from my brief glance, is thousands of English language students and a general air of prosperity. There is no racing on that day – only cricket at the College – but when my mate, usually a pint of bitter man, goes to the National Hunt Festival, he sets aside a champagne budget.

No wonder they bristle with resentment in Gloucester. They do have a chuckle, though, at the misconceptions of visitors, who imagine that the city is some sort of extension to the Cotswolds, all huntin', fishin' and shootin'. Actually, they do have the occasional shooting in the badlands of the city centre, so one out three isn't bad. And then there's Fred West, still casting a shadow decades after his crimes, in a way only matched by my original home town of Hyde, which produced both the Moors Murderers and Dr Harold Shipman. There's even a Gloucester compass; North, South, East and We Don't Talk About That One.

What they do talk about at some length in the Linden Tree is what a no-account place Gloucester is. The exception is Steve, a freelance pilot from Devon, who chooses to spend his midweeks in Gloucester, although most of his work is in and around Bristol. Apparently you can't get a bed and breakfast there for love nor money, mainly because of the shifting population of the aeronautical industry. He has a block booking at the pub and you could do a lot worse; big plates of unpretentious food and a full range of beers from Wadworths of Devizes. You don't even have to join in with the ritual slagging-off of Gloucester, if you don't feel like it.

Christopher Winn's *I Never Knew That About England* puts the case for the defence succinctly: 'Gloucestershire's county town is often compared unfavourably to Cheltenham or Tewkesbury, although it is older and more hard working than both.'

Part of the problem, it occurs to me, is the name. Gloucester has the Shire suffix to live up to. (Suffix? I hear you implore. Yes, a fictional county somewhere between Suffolk and Sussex or is it Suffolk and Essex?). There seems to be some sort of frustrated expectation that the city should be the apotheosis of all things Gloucestershire. If the county was called Bristolshire, or Chipping Sodburyshire, or even Cheltenhamshire, the pressure would be off and Gloucester could just get on with it.

Besides, it wasn't Cheltenham that Dr Foster went to. It was poor old Gloster and, far from never going there again, he might have had trouble ever leaving.

IT should be perfectly simple. You're on the main road to Bristol with a bus stop right in front of the pub; how difficult can it be to get a bus to Bristol?

The answer, after another slap-up breakfast, served in the skittle alley – mercifully not in use, but still a personal first – is very difficult indeed. There are plenty of buses to a place called Quedgeley, which sounds made up to me, one a week to Thornbury, near Bristol, via the bird sanctuary at Slimbridge, and the occasional one marked 'Sorry. Not in Service. Try Cheltenham.' Fortunately, I have a cunning plan.

I calculate that, if I get a bus towards Dursley but get off before the village, I should be able to catch one to Thornbury on the way out. I'm not too worried about missing out on the delights of downtown Dursley. JK Rowling, who comes from nearby Yate, thought it was so dull that she called the dullest family in the whole *Harry Potter* saga by the same name.

As we go through a village called either Cam or Lower Cam, though – I'm not sure of the distinction – I get a funny feeling, an itch in my bus pass pocket, an idea that I should get off there and then. At first, I think I might have made a blunder and will have to trudge defeated into Dursley, but there, around the next bend, ticking over as if it's waiting just for me, is a bus marked 'Thornbury for Bristol' and yes, it's going all the way. It's something that happens quite a lot in the West Country; you get to travel the advertised route and then there's a little bonus at the end. This bus turns off the main drag almost as soon as I've sat down and if I'd been a minute earlier or a minute later I would have missed it. I call that a triumph for intuition.

The road into Bristol is notable for two things. There's the sheer extent of the aerospace industry that, among other things, brings Steve and his ilk to Gloucestershire every week. Bristol always seems to have found a way to make money, be it from slaves, tobacco or missiles.

Then there's the melting pot of bars, restaurants, cafés and shops, reflecting more nationalities than you can shake a stick at, lining Gloucester Road as you come into the city. I don't remember it being like that when I was a regular visitor in the 1970s – it looks a lot more fun now. Indeed, it claims to be the longest stretch of independent businesses in the country.

In Bristol, my infallible instincts let me down slightly, as I schlep across the city to Temple Meads station to catch a bus I could have caught at the bus station where I'd arrived. Still, it gave me chance to contemplate what must be one of the most ornate railway stations in the world. The humble bus to Wells leaves from a stop just down the street. Two young women, with pushchairs loaded down with infants and shopping, get off at the idyllic-sounding village of Temple Cloud.

On the other side of the Mendips, Wells itself is one of those curiously out-of-scale places in which Britain abounds. Its huge cathedral makes it England's smallest city; indeed, it would qualify as one of its smaller towns, as well as one of its more beautiful ones. It has plenty of visitors, though, and a bustling bus station. But there is trouble in paradise. One of the drivers is seeking out everyone planning to travel on his bus and telling them that he can't take them to one section of the route, because the road up the hill is blocked by parked cars. I thought it might be something to do with the Glastonbury Festival, the monstrously overgrown gig that began 10 days hence. But no, the problem was that residents – or maybe weekend residents – had parked their 4x4s in stupid places. There ensued an illuminating little chat between three bus drivers about how it was possible to nip off a wing mirror, clean as a whistle, in a way that looked accidental. Be warned, inconsiderate parkers.

In a few miles, you get a fine, long-distance view of Glastonbury Tor, the focus of so much mystical mumbo-jumbo, followed by the town itself, which is full of the sort of shops you would expect it to be full of. Macrobiotic crystals, anyone? The festival isn't at Tor or town, but in a farmer's field some distance away. The Pilton Farm Festival doesn't have the same ring about it at all.

A little further on, not far from the village of Oath, where the air is presumably always blue, there is a humpback bridge, possibly with a trickle of water in the ditch below. This is the mighty River Parrett, the Yangtse of the Somerset Levels, which terrorised and inundated half the county the previous winter. Now you could barely moisten a postage stamp in it.

IT was in a mood of stoical self-sacrifice that I rode the number 376 into the county town of Taunton. In the spirit of 'when in Rome, do as the Romanians do,' I had resolved to spend a day drinking nothing but cider. This was that fateful day and I hadn't been looking forward to it.

I'd always been suspicious of cider; at 15, I got disastrously drunk on it at the Sidmouth Folk Festival and it hadn't tasted right since; I still have a similar problem with ouzo, but that's another story.

Nor are people who have devoted a lifetime to drinking cider a particularly good advert for it. Bolton's number one celebrity drunk and vagrant was Cider Billy; not Real Ale Billy or Gin and Tonic Billy, you note, but Cider Billy. On the other hand, Laurie Lee – the great writer from these parts, for my money – enjoyed *Cider With Rosie*, not Carlsberg Special Brew With Rosie, so each to his own, perhaps. What can't be denied is that, if you come across a couple of drinkers arguing violently, the chances are that they have been on the cider. Wherever it is drunk in quantity, there will be men talking absolute bollocks. It must be something in the apples. Or maybe not; the friend of a friend was organising some promotional activity on behalf of a well-known brand and suggested that the apple should be given more prominence.

'Better not,' he was told, 'there aren't any actual apples in it.'

That wasn't the stuff I was trying; I was on the cloudy tackle with cores, branches, roots and heaven knows what else in it. I gave it my best shot, if that is not mixing my drinks excessively, although I was drinking halves. I might have had eight in Bristol, Wells and Taunton and I can't remember any names; I was taking notes, but I spilled some cider on them and they shrivelled up like a 300-year-old treasure map or a neglected scrap torn off the *Mappa Mundi*. I knew it was time to pack it in when I started arguing with myself. (On no, I didn't. And what the hell do you know about it, you pisshead?) I have to admit that the taste improved as the controlled experiment progressed. By the end, it tasted almost as good as beer that had gone off. That's the best I can do and you're welcome to use it in your advertising.

I had hoped to see some cricket in Taunton, so I was

chuffed when I heard someone was playing at the County Ground. Unfortunately, it turned out to be Rod Stewart and I wasn't forking out fifty quid to see him turn his arm over.

Instead, I settled for a wander. For a relatively small place, Taunton seems to have at least three town centres. I had the feeling I was in the wrong one, but did find a Tardis of an Indian restaurant – which, like a Chinese I happened upon in Hereford, hid a massive interior behind a small doorway. I think this whole expedition would be impossible without England's Oriental feeding stations and I washed my lamb, spinach and aubergine down with a cider. Only kidding, with a beer.

I WAS prepared for trouble in Taunton. A few weeks earlier, the specialist bus press – yes, there is such a thing – had run an alarming story that Devon was stopping accepting bus passes on some of its popular tourist-orientated routes.

Their rationale was that they were seasonal, rather than regular services and thus not covered by the legislation. It sounds to me like the thin end of a very big wedge and the possible launch of a West Country UDI or a new Monmouth Rebellion. What should we do about it? Boycott their clotted cream?

The route that affected me was the one from Taunton to Minehead, Lynmouth and Ilfracombe, squeezing between Exmoor and the sea. The problem seemed to be that old people were virtually living on it, getting off only to recharge their thermos flasks and Tupperware sandwich boxes.

Old people are incorrigible; you don't fully realise

how incorrigible until you become one yourself. There was an alternative route through Tiverton, with no restrictions on the bus pass, but that only concealed a fiendish trap. Imagine, you arrive at the bus station to confirm that you can't take the coast road. Never mind, says the kindly driver, there's another route.

'And when does that leave?' you ask.

'Five minutes ago,' says he.

Oh, how they must have laughed at that one down at the depot. Fortunately, I'm wise to this and head straight for the Tiverton and Barnstaple service, driven by a ruddy-cheeked West Countryman, straight from Central Casting.

'Aaar Barns'ple, aar,' he says. 'Orl the way!'

Which is good enough for me. I'm sure the coast route is a scenic delight, if you can see out of the window through the steam from pensioners' tea, but it can't be all that much better than the inland route. Once through Wellington, it leads through a series of twisting country lanes, many so overhung by trees that it is like travelling through leafy tunnels. At other stages, you pop out into the open like a cork from a green bottle and you have a view across six little valleys. Minehead must be crafted out of solid gold by cherubim and seraphim, if it's so superior to this. Remarkably, it's all being negotiated in a double-decker, with our mate, the driver, occasionally throwing in a burst of mock-dramatic commentary, like: 'I durn't know if we'll make this.'

The most startling change of scene comes just outside Tiverton when we suddenly emerge from a forest into the middle of a public school, with floppy-haired youths in striped blazers and girls carrying bags full of books on both sides of the road. This is Blundell's School (established 1604, annual fees £28,200) whose rugby-playing alumni include

Clem Thomas and Richard Sharp, as well as RD Blackmore, who wrote *Lorna Doone*. I don't think that's the same Richie Blackmore who played centre for Castleford and New Zealand, but he could be some distant kin to Mike Blackmore, a Devonian who signed for Hull KR. It is not in danger of being confused with the local comprehensive.

Neighbours-without-Harbours

THE road to Barnstaple offers views of Exmoor to the right and, more distantly, the outline of Dartmoor to the left.

It is a more restful landscape than either, tucked there between them, and I think I must have nodded off, because suddenly we are in the outskirts of Barnstaple, another of those places with an ancient claim to fame – in this case as the first borough in England in AD 930 – and one which used to issue its own coins. Its importance disappeared when its harbour silted up in the 19th century. Maybe it was the first cloud of the week blotting out the sun, maybe I was still half asleep, but I took a mild but instant dislike to Barnstaple. I could see no pubs, nor, once we got to the gloomy little bus station, any guest houses. What I could see was a bus stop marked Bideford. In the tourist information office, they were rushing to close before anyone could ask them a question. I had a bad feeling about the place and the Bideford bus was revving up.

Getting aboard was one of the better decisions I've made of late. You follow the Rivers Taw and Torridge to a place called East-the-Water; set that alongside Westward Ho! (don't forget the !) a couple of miles away and it sounds like a pair of cider drinkers arguing about directions. To complicate

61

the argument further, Charles Kingsley wrote the novel, *Westward Ho!*, in East-the-Water. It opens up a whole new field of study – punctuation marks in place names. Of places we've visited so far, I'd suggest (Gloucester) and Ross on Wye? And of ones we miss, Batley's home: Mount 'Pleasant'.

You cross the Torridge on a long, low bridge and you're in Bideford. First impressions are not brilliant; a boarded-up hotel that must once have been the town's biggest. But then you're on the quayside and in an immediately likeable place.

My good pal, Bernard Wrigley, has written a song called 'Bideford Harbour'. It's a catchy little number about all the exotic cargoes from the seven seas being unloaded at said harbour. Just one snag – Bideford doesn't have a harbour. What it has is a tidal quay and that is a very different thing. Modestly sized vessels – fishing boats, coastal freighters, the Lundy Island ferry – can tie up there, but the QE2 and container ships from Rotterdam? I'm afraid not, Bernard.

I have to report that he is unrepentant.

'Sod 'em,' he says. 'Bideford Quay doesn't scan.'

The first pub I try for a room, the King's Arms, is full, but they just about take me by the hand and lead me to the information office. They fix me up at a bed and breakfast up the road and would have carried me there shoulder high if I'd let them. Mind you, it helps when you announce your arrival by bad mouthing the local rivals. If you can honestly say that you took one look at Barnstaple and got on the bus to Bideford, you've got friends for life. I go back to the pub for fish and chips at a table on the quayside and I can't believe that Rick Stein himself could have done it better. Washed down with a couple of pints of Golden Pig, from the Country Life Brewery, next to Bideford's Big Sheep landmark, it is fit for a king.

My B&B is close to Bideford FC's ground. Biddy, or

the Pride of North Devon as they call themselves, are in the Southern League, whilst Barnstaple Town (Barum) are in the Western, but the websites of both clubs claim that they have 'a friendly rivalry' with each other. I bet they do; the sort of rivalry that makes my little atlas mark the body of water where the Torridge and the Taw meet the sea as Barnstaple Bay OR Bideford Bay. You can call it either, but for heaven's sake remember where you are. I had the most pleasant of evenings strolling around the town's backstreet pubs. If I'd kept mentioning my Escape from Barnstaple in conversation, I would have been on free ale all night.

THIS always looked like a complicated day and, sure enough, it was, starting on a double-decker on Bideford Quay and zigging and zagging via Bude, Okehampton and Wadebridge towards the promised land of Padstow.

Okehampton is notable for the number of Asian ladies of all ages doing their shopping. Okay, maybe half a dozen, but in Okehampton that looks like quite a lot. In the pub up the street, the staff and customers are nearly collapsing from the heat. We have reached that stage, about three days into a heatwave, when the English start to gasp 'Enough ... enough. It was alright at first, but now we've had enough.' Or the woman I heard pleading on the 501 on a warmish day: 'If I black out before we get there, put me off at Campbell Street.'

Near the appropriately named village of Welcombe, we cross the Cornish frontier. Sadly, a diversion to Port Isaac, home of the celebrated shantymen, the Fishermen's Friends, would have turned a complicated day into an impossible one. When I phoned the Golden Lion in Padstow at the start of May, it sounded as though the World Cup – my constant companion on the first leg of this journey – had already started and was being played in their public bar.

'Sorry,' a voice on the end of the line shouted above the din. 'Can you phone back when we're not as busy? And the credit card machine's gone missing. It's bedlam in here.'

It was nine o'clock in the morning – a little early for uncontrollable merriment, even in Cornwall. And then it struck me. It was May 1 – 'Obby 'Oss Day.

The 'Obby 'Oss, a large, decorated figure that leads the crowds through the streets of the town in Britain's most famous May Day celebration, lives in the Golden Lion, where I make my booking when the excitement has died down a little. I think the town's attitude to visitors has warmed a little in recent years. Joe Boyd, in his autobiography *White Bicycles*, recalls going there for 'Obby 'Oss day in the early-60s and seeing a BBC film-crew having its equipment dumped in the harbour when they showed just a little too much interest in the ceremonial.

The other thing Padstow is famous for is the Rick Stein seafood empire. The TV chef has a number of outlets in the town, ranging from arm-and-a-leg expensive to almost affordable, if not exactly cheap and cheerful. I head for what might be termed the Rick Stein Chippy.

One thing it doesn't have is a Uruguayan restaurant. A Montevideo Bar and Grill on the harbour from which tens of thousands of Cornishmen, mainly tin miners, embarked for new lives in the Americas and Australia, would have solved my World Cup viewing issues – I had to watch England versus Uruguay – at a stroke. After a bout of selfless research,

I settle for the front bar at the Golden Lion, where a previously inconspicuous flat screen TV is lunging out in front of the dart board. The bar's attempts to encourage / disparage England's performance have a distinct Cornish flavour. In fact, the worse England get, the more Cornish the Golden Lion becomes.

'Don't pass it to he!' one viewer screams at the screen and before long we're all at it, oohing and aahing at the very occasional highlights. 'You wazzock, Johnson!'

When I retire to my bedroom, a thing that looks like a little robot appears at my window and starts spraying liquid around. It turns out not to be an attempted alien abduction, but an automated watering system for the pub's window boxes and hanging baskets, which are so many and various that parts of the building are completely obscured by flowers.

I knew I was going to like Padstow. Anywhere built on the twin foundations of incomprehensible ritual and fresh fish has to be okay by me. As for any ambitions to dine with Stein, or at least to eat at his top of the range restaurant, however, forget it. His main place is advertising a bargain lunch at £38.50; you can buy a whole chippy in Hull for that.

Helston: England's Deep South

IT's another day of complicated travel to get to Helston, starting with the 09.36am number 556 to Newquay being diverted miles off its normal route because of a road closure on the way out of Padstow.

We enter Newquay, a place of which I have idyllic memories of an early-teenaged holiday spent almost entirely in the surf, through the tradesman's entrance, seeing not the sea but the scruffy, impermanent looking streets behind it. It looks like one of the more downmarket surf resorts in Australia, but not in a good way. There is a reminder in the early autumn, though, that it can be as dangerous as anywhere else with breakers, when three surfers die at one of the town's beaches.

From Newquay , it's another bus to St Columb Major, not to be mixed up with St Columb Minor, which is several miles away, or St Columb Road, which is, fittingly, just down the road. This is an introduction to a potential minefield; the issue of confusing Cornish names – or Cornfusion for short. Apart from the columns of St Columbs, there's St Just, St Just in Roseland, St Just Outside Roseland and St Just Nowhere Near Roseland.

Then there's the lost tribe of Ts, where you don't know where the West Country place names stop and the county cricketers begin: Truro, Tresco, Trego, Tesco, Trevarrick, Trescothick. It reads like a very, very irregular Latin verb. The other thing I notice, checking my current edition map of the tip of Cornwall, is that a previous owner has sprinkled it with neat, pencilled crosses at strategic points on the landscape. I waste an hour trying to work out what they might be; instructions for an invasion that never happened, perhaps.

For a place of its modest size – around 10,000 – Helston has plenty of claims to fame. Officially the most southerly town on the British mainland, it also has the most southerly sporting hero. Bob Fitzsimmons was world heavyweight boxing champion and the first Briton to hold the title when he knocked out 'Gentleman' Jim Corbett in 1897. Actually, he and his family emigrated to New Zealand when he was nine, but Helston clings tenaciously to its claim on him and there's a plaque on the thatched cottage that was his childhood home to underline it.

Fitzsimmons was all of 11st 2in when he won the title; considerably less than either Froch or Groves, or about half a Klitschko brother. He used to wear heavy woollen shorts in the ring to disguise his thin legs and even his nickname sounds unlikely to strike terror – The Freckled Wonder. It's not exactly Carl 'The Cobra' Froch or James 'Bonecrusher' Smith, but apparently he had a punch like a kick from a Cornish pit pony.

What you need to remember in this little town is not to get into any arguments with freckly men with thin legs.

Other reasons for coming to Helston include the Furry Dance, traditionally held a week after the jollifications in Padstow and made infamous by Terry Wogan as the Floral Dance, and the Blue Anchor, which was once one of only four pubs left in Britain brewing its own beer; two of the others were in Shropshire.

It would be rude not to stay there and it deserves every bit of its legendary status. It's a warren of shady little rooms – dingy, you could call them if you wanted to be picky – with a central bar selling the famous Spingo beers, brewed on the premises since heaven knows when. Just in case that's not enough, there's a beer festival in the back garden. They have taken over the Georgian terrace next door for the bed and breakfast side of the business and I have a big room with a large bow window, looking up and down Coinagehall Street. You hear a lot of complaints that 'High Streets' everywhere in Britain are a) deeply depressed and b) indistinguishable from each other. However next door to the Blue Anchor is a stationer/newsagent/tobacconist proudly advertising two of its best lines: Extra thin pipe-cleaners and Rose petal wedding confetti; not forgetting the *Helston Packet* weekly paper. Find me an exact match for that stocklist at WH Smith if you can, anywhere in the country.

There might be a corner shop somewhere with bog-standard thick pipe-cleaners and confetti modelled on something other than rose-petals, but somehow I doubt it.

You'll have to go to Helston.

The longest day

IT is outside that very shop that I'm waiting for the bus to Penzance bright and early the following morning.

It happens to be June 21, longest day of the year. Given that we're in the most southerly town in mainland Britain, this is the most summer that you can experience without getting your feet wet. Small wonder that there are all manner of festivities planned for later; probably including a few sacrifices to the Sun God. The Scots do even better, of course, playing midnight golf on courses where the sun scarcely sets.

Isn't it barmy, though, that you can truthfully say on June 22, when the previous winter's snows are just thawing on the Pennines, that the nights are drawing in? Midsummer comes before summer has really started in most years. It's a very negative message and it's bad for the psychology of the nation. The solution? Simple really; just wind the clocks forward an hour on Midsummer Day, as a sort of solstice bonus.

There is rather a striking woman, with green and purple highlights in her fine grey hair, also waiting for the bus. She is going to Penzance, to try to sell the house she owns there, but she isn't optimistic. I tell her that I would have thought that any house around there would be a pretty saleable proposition and she makes a game attempt to sell it to me, right there in the bus queue.

I'm not really in the market for a holiday home in Cornwall, but, if I were, I would cheerfully pay a premium for a view of St Michael's Mount when I open my curtains in the morning. To get that, you need to be in the village of Marazion on Mounts Bay, a couple of miles before Penzance. There or in Normandy, where there is the matching Mont St Michel. There is another Land's End as well; Finisterre in Galicia, which used to be a shipping forecast area, but is now known, rather prosaically, as Fitzroy.

In Penzance itself, the Land's End bus is revving up and I'm delighted to find that it's an open top job.

They could easily charge extra for this trip, on the basis that tourists are fair game, but they don't. Nor do they worry too much about health and safety considerations. You're okay at the front of upper deck, where you are protected from overhanging branches by a windscreen, but further back you are at their mercy. I do my share of bobbing and weaving, but still get caught with a couple of glancing blows. It would only need one kid to be bobbing when they should be weaving and be taken to hospital and that will be the end of the open-topped bus to Land's End. Experience it, killer branches and all, while you can.

Although it's the only time in the first 500 miles of this jaunt that I wear my hoody, it's a glorious midsummer's day and the views are sensational as we twist along narrow lanes between tiny villages. It's just a shame that it finishes at Land's End – although you are entitled to ask what else it could do there.

A series of unsympathetic owners have ruined the most westerly point of the British mainland by turning it into a theme park, when all you really need is a path down onto the rocks. It is so dispiriting that I don't even get off the bus, although mild concussion might have something to do with that. On the way back to Penzance, however, there are two places worth stopping the bus for. One is the Minack Theatre, carved out of the south-facing cliffs just around the corner from Land's End; a setting in which I would even be prepared to watch *Waiting for Godot* again, without a gun to my head. The other is the miniscule nearby village of Porthcurno, which is where the submarine cable that linked the world's communications together came ashore. Hard to imagine now, but through this hamlet passed messages to the furthest flung corners of the British Empire. I send a message of my own home on the mobile phone that is today's equivalent miracle; I've turned the corner and I'm on the way home. Sort of.

Apart from Land's End, I'm in pursuit of another Cornish icon on Midsummer's Day – the pasty. The distinctively shaped baked snack is so ubiquitous now that it needs the Cornish in front of the pasty to remind us of its origins. Those were supposedly in the tin mines, where the miners needed a durable meal they could carry down with them. Today the tin mines, tomorrow the world, because you can buy a 'Cornish' pasty anywhere in the world, probably including the North and South Poles and Everest Base Camp. It must surely be possible, therefore, to subsist in Cornwall on pasties and nothing else for 24 hours. Lunch, tea and supper present no problems; Penzance, Truro and Bodmin are all as pasty-friendly as you would expect. The pasties themselves share one characteristic; the meat, potato and vegetables are virtually separate. Cornish pasty-makers feel under no compunction about layering their ingredients, rather than mixing them all together as you would do further north. Perhaps this is a hang-over from the fabled two-course pasty of the tin mines, with jam or apple at one end. I never saw one of these specimens on my travels and I'm tempted to dismiss them as an urban myth.

In any case, I'm out of the race by then, like one of those loose horses in the Grand National that dumps its rider at the first fence but carries on running. The trouble was that there appears to be no such thing as a breakfast pasty.

This isn't as weird as it sounds. The Australians, whose love of a pie exceeds even that of Wiganers, have an egg and bacon variety that does the job perfectly, but there is no pasty equivalent. What they do have, by way of distinctive breakfast fare, is hogs pudding, which is neither the Northern English black pudding nor the Scottish white pudding, but a type of small pork rissole. A couple of them and the rest of the day on pasties and I reckon I've paid my gastronomic dues to the Duchy.

To say that getting out of Cornwall in what remained of Midsummer's Day was a little complicated would be a severe understatement. The first barriers to progress are the twin towns of Camborne and Redruth – Cornwall's ugly sisters. They squat beside the A30 like two big dollops of reality in an enchanted land and I can't begin to describe to you where one ends and the other begins.

I went for a walk around one of them and there was an atmosphere I recognised; essence of closed-down mining town. In fact, if you come from the North of England to West Cornwall there are several points of reference, like the three Ms – mines, moors and Methodism. The weather's better, though.

The particular brand of depression in Cornwall springs from the death not of one industry but two – tin and china clay. The clay has left white spoil tips near St Austell which gleam spectacularly in the sun and are one of the county's unlikelier tourist attractions. Tourism goes only a small way towards filling the gap created by dead industries, though, and it can leave the tourist, especially ones carrying a free bus pass, feeling slightly uneasy at times. For instance, there am I, escaping from Camborne (or Redruth) and generally zigging and zagging across the county for fun and for free, whilst it is costing a family with three kids about 15 quid to go into the nearest town and back. It's easy for me to say now, because I've already benefitted from this largesse, but you are bound to wonder whether the subsidies are going to the right places.

I say zigging and zagging because a route through Truro, Bodmin, St Austell and Liskeard is about as straight and direct as a corkscrew. Finally, on my seventh bus of the day, we cross the River Tamar into Devon, with a regatta going on at Saltash on the Cornish side of the bridge.

On my first visit for almost 50 years, I've enjoyed Cornwall a lot. There have been some changes; the Cornish language has gone from officially extinct to merely nearly extinct and you see a lot more of the Cornish flag. With its white cross on a black background, it looks vaguely piratical, or like one of the paper flags you used to stick in sandcastles.

Of full-fledged Cornish nationalism, though, not a sign, although there is an activist with the too-good-to-invent name of Dr Loveday Jenkin. Nor, as I leave the Duchy, is there any trace of jam-filled pasties, although, if they did exist, they could be the answer to the breakfast question.

GOING NORTH

PLYMOUTH and Exeter are one of those pairs of cities that, from a distance, you tend to bracket together and assume that they must have excellent transport links between them. This is not true, in my experience, of doing it by bus.

At Plymouth bus station, they have difficulty in believing that anyone could want to go to Exeter and can offer me little advice on how to do it. I notice that one of the exits is labelled Exeter Street and decide that it might point in the approximate direction of Exeter. Sure enough, there is a bus shelter across the road, occupied by a drunk with a bottle of Buckfast in a brown paper bag. I know it's Buckfast because he removes it triumphantly from its bag, points at the label, belches and offers me a swig.

I decline politely. There's no way of being sure, but he could well be a Scot, because 'a wee Buckie' – a sweet fortified wine – has long been a favourite chaser for the serious Scottish drinker. It is made by the monks at Buckfast Abbey, half-way to Exeter; the second item in the South West news on TV that very day had been the visit of the Archbishop of Canterbury to the abbey. Probably taking back the empties. They have a similar thing about Benedictine in East

Lancashire, but that dates back to the First World War, and very comforting in the trenches it must have been.

A bus to Ivybridge arrives. It's a mere quarter of the way to Exeter, right at the southern tip of the Dartmoor National Park, but better than nothing. As I'm getting on and fumbling for my pass, though, a bus for Totnes and Paignton zooms past. That would have been a much better option and I'm cursing my luck.

'Not to worry,' says the driver. 'I reckon I can catch him before Ivybridge.'

He's as good as his word. In fact, he seems to relish a bit of a challenge towards the end of his working day. After some Hamilton and Rosberg-style duelling and overtaking, he deposits me at the bus stop in Ivybridge a couple of minutes before the Paignton bus arrives and I tell him he's a hero.

Paignton had not been on my planned itinerary, but at the end of The Longest Day, it would do perfectly well. I wandered up a side-street off the front and found a hotel. It might be possible to stay in a place like this, in this part of the world, without hearing echoes of *Fawlty Towers* but it would take a stronger man than me. All the familiar comic ingredients were there; the brittle over-anxiety to please, the accident prone guests, the inevitable misunderstandings.

As I booked in, there was an elderly couple checking out, after the man had cut himself quite badly in a fall and needed hospital treatment. Somebody else was on the phone and the proprietress was telling them: 'I'm most terribly sorry. I really don't know how that can have happened. I checked it the other day.' There was another minor casualty to deal with before she got round to me.

'Can you write, dear?' she asked me.

'Well, I like to think so,' I said, mentally scanning a

modest shelf of books with my name on the spine. 'I've not done too badly.'

She gave me a funny look and I realised that she was inquiring whether I could physically hold a pen, because nobody else in that foyer could.

The following morning, I dodge the columns of the walking wounded and catch the bus to Torquay. At Teignmouth, there is a poignant notice on the Baptist church, inviting people to come and watch the World Cup games in a 'family-friendly atmosphere.' Next to the town's bus stops there is a folk festival going on, with several sets of morris dancers doing their thing. Tempted to get off and join in, but worried about the scarcity of buses on a Sunday.

Dawlish, on the other hand, had always been on my essential calling list, because of its starring role in the previous winter's floods. Other towns had their roads inundated; Dawlish had its railway line washed away.

Six months later, you can imagine how. The line virtually runs along the beach and looks like a bit of over-enthusiastic bucket and spade work could bring it down again. You can go under the line to a little café and sit there mulling over the fragility of the arrangements and accommodations we have made with the waters that surround us. Dawlish has tidied itself up pretty nicely since the floods – it took just eight weeks to get the rail line up and running again - but the tourist business must have taken a real kicking. That has left the town in danger of sending out mixed messages to the rest of the world. 'Things are really, really bad here,' they say, 'but don't let that put you off booking in for a couple of weeks in July.'

Coming into Exeter, there is the surprising sight of a small gunship crossing the road on the Exeter Canal, while the bus waits for the bridge to swing back into position. It's into Exeter and straight out again for me, because I'm anticipating a top time in Topsham.

TOPSHAM – or Topsum to its inhabitants – is only four miles from Exeter, but it is a different world. It was once famous for its shipbuilding. The Terror, one of Sir John Franklin's two ill-fated ships that attempted to find the North West Passage around the top of Canada in 1845, was built here. The ships were caught and crushed in the ice, with all 129 on board presumed dead. The Canadians have recently found a ship that must be one or the other. If it's The Terror, it's testimony to the quality of Topsham shipbuilding, because, apart from the inevitable damage done by the icy embrace of an Arctic winter from which they were too late to extricate themselves, it is still in pretty good condition.

So is Topsham these days, after a period of neglect in the 1960s. It's now cherished for its distinctive architecture and laid-back atmosphere. My bed and breakfast is in the big house that used to belong to the doctor and is full of early 20th century detail. It claims to serve the best cream teas in Devon, but I'm boycotting them since that nasty business of the Exmoor bus. Instead, I sit outside a pub on the quayside, have a plate of assorted fish and watch people variously messing about on the water.

All very pleasant, but it's not what I'm here for. You have to walk a mile or so out of town for that, where a steep hill drops down to the weir on the River Clyst and the Bridge Inn comes into view. Topsham has other distinctions – it was home to Dick Pym, Bolton Wanderers' goalkeeper in the first-ever Wembley FA Cup final in 1923, to the newsreader, Sir Trevor McDonald, and still is to the folk group, Show of Hands – but the Bridge is what makes it worth a detour.

This was my third attempt. Twice before, I'd lobbed up on the doorstep and found it resolutely locked and barred. The trouble was that this most traditional of pubs sticks rigidly to pre-liberalisation opening hours, which, lest we forget, means 12 noon to 2.00pm and 7.00pm to 10.30pm on a Sunday, for instance, and not much more than that during the week.

That isn't the only thing about the Bridge that is out of its time. It also has no truck with new-fangled innovations like a bar or beer pumps. What it has instead is a serving-hatch leading into the family's sitting room, from which they go down into the cellar, fill your glass by gravity from one of a variety of barrels and bring it back up the stairs to you. At one time, most country pubs would have been like this; now, it is unique.

It has also been in the same family for 111 years and they run it this way, not because of some ingrained Luddism nor to contrive a bogus retro mood, but simply because it suits them and, they believe, their customers. The current licensee, the fourth in the family line, is Caroline Cheffers-Heard and she says that if she had opened longer hours she would have packed it in long before now. Besides, she gently chides me, I could have looked up the Stone Age opening hours on – yes, irony warning coming up – the internet. You can now also check which beers are on stillage in the same way. The Bridge isn't divorced from the modern world, it just defines its own relationship with it on its own terms.

It also knows the value of publicity. It claims to be the only pub in the country to be visited by that well-known real ale enthusiast, HM The Queen, who 'popped in' in 1998. She probably thinks all the pubs in her realm are like this. A long-delayed return invitation came in 2014, when Caroline was summoned to Buckingham Palace as a representative of the hospitality industry. You can imagine the conversation: 'Does one still have Branscombe Vale Branoc in one's cellar?' They still do, but no lager, no piped music and no television – and, of course, no fly-by-night gimmicks like a bar.

At breakfast the following morning at my digs the talk is all about an apparent attempt at a break-in overnight. I suspect that was me, coming back from a convivial evening at the Bridge and trying to negotiate the old doctor's original 19th century system of locks and bolts. I managed it in the end, but I could well believe that I sounded like a band of very clumsy and ultimately easily deterred burglars.

The lady serving the bacon and sausages – all from local farms and butchers – has found out that I'm from Bolton, a place with which she has family connections and occasionally visits.

'You know the biggest difference I notice?' she says. 'There's a lot more coloured people. We don't have many coloured people in Exeter.'

What about Trevor McDonald? I'm tempted to splutter through the toast and coffee like an apopleptic Brian Blessed, but I feel sure she's angling for some sort of confirmation of how difficult that makes life in the north. I wonder whether to throw the curve ball of my three half-Asian nephews and nieces, but in the end I just eat my breakfast.

To the naked eye, the West Country is astonishingly homogenous. The most visible minority consists of the oriental wives and partners of West Countrymen, especially on the coast. No doubt they all have their individual stories of how they come to be there, but a typical arrangement might be a pub or restaurant with the man glad-handing and drinking with his mates at the front of house and the woman working away in the kitchen; East meets West.

THERE are some epic bus routes in Britain. In England, you can get a single bus between Peterborough and Lowestoft, two towns which can barely know of each other's existence, or Newcastle and Keswick, both of which I am scheduled to sample later in this journey.

Wales has the marathon route linking Newtown with Cardiff, but it's hard to beat the X53, which runs from Exeter to Poole and which, with all its twists and turns, must weigh in at close to 100 miles. It's timetabled to take 4 hours and 40 minutes if you stay on board all the way, although taking a break somewhere en route is a much better idea.

The X53 advertises itself as running along the Jurassic Coast, which isn't quite the case. There isn't a continuous road that runs alongside the sea and could take a double-decker bus. So the X53 does a good deal of ducking and diving, dropping into coastal towns and villages and climbing out again; hence the 4 hours 40 minutes. All the same, it's a magnificent trip, as well as being, at 0 pounds and 0 pence, one of the world's great travel bargains for all us old fossils. No wonder it's the closest I've come so far to a full bus.

The Jurassic Coast is so called because of the erosion of its cliffs to reveal the fossil-rich strata beneath. Its marketing is predictably heavy with dinosaurs; indeed, my younger grandchildren were convinced at one stage that I was actually going to see pterodactyls, rather than the occasional angry seagull. Our first close encounter with the sea is at the inspiringly named village of Beer and again at Lyme Regis, which is now officially a place to visit, following the success of the film of John Fowles' *The French Lieutenant's Woman*, with Meryl Streep emoting on The Cobb – the town's photogenic harbour wall – like a life insurance advert. The Cobb figures as well in Jane Austen's *Persuasion* and we are also deep in Thomas Hardy's Wessex. Hardy constructed a whole parallel gazetteer for the area, with thinly-veiled pseudonyms like Casterbridge for Dorchester and Port Bredy for Bridport. Curiously, Lyme Regis is Lyme Regis.

In any case, Hardy the novelist is much more a chronicler of the interior than of the coast; inward rather than outward looking. The rogue sheepdogs driving the flock of sheep over the cliff in *Far from the Madding Crowd* are one of the exceptions. Hardy the poet, as he primarily saw himself, was more of a maritime man. Take the description of the English Channel in sympathetically furious mood on the Dorset coast as the Battle of Trafalgar raged, several sea areas away.

> In the wild October night-time, the wind raved
> round the land,
> And the back-sea met the front-sea and our
> doors were blocked with sand.
>
> 'The Night of Trafalgar'

When the weather is set fair and the sea is rippling gently, it's as well to remember what it can be like; indeed, what it was like a few months earlier. This is one of those sections of the English coast where you can become genuinely concerned about the country crumbling away and shrinking. Walk along a clifftop path now and, if you go back a couple of years later, it's gone. That's the lie of the land on the Isle of Wight, for instance, and in parts of Cleveland and North Yorkshire. Instead of catching 100-odd buses, should I just have sat tight and waited for the coast to come to me?

It is pleasing to be able to report in passing that the leader of Dorset County Council, the man who makes all the statements about how difficult it is protecting the coast and running country bus services, glories in the impeccably Hardyesque name of Spencer Flower. He is councillor for Verwood and Three Legged Cross, of all the catchily named constituencies. Either Lyme Regis or Bridport would have served perfectly well for breaking the journey, but I stayed on for a couple of miles to West Bay.

This is another place used as a backdrop for fiction, in this case the popular TV series *Broadchurch*. My son's mate works in television and was involved in finding locations there. I can understand how it caught his eye. With its massive cliff overhanging its shelving, stony beach, there's a brooding atmosphere about the place, softened only by the family bustle around the seafood stalls on the harbour.

Talking of impressive cliffs, though, I suppose that, before I set out, I presumed that the high spots on the South Coast would be Beachy Head, or possibly the bluebird infested White Cliffs of Dover. Wrong, wrong, wrong; the highest point is somewhere I had never heard of – Golden Cap, between Lyme Regis and West Bay, soaring to 191 metres, with glorious views of Chesil Beach and the Isle of Portland. That was where I once went to interview the rugby league immortal, Brian Bevan, for my first book, almost 30 years earlier. After his legendary playing days, he was a military policeman at Portland and nobody had the faintest idea who he was.

Route 63

The route side-steps Dorchester, with all its Hardy connections. I wonder whether people living there feel themselves particularly at the mercy of Fate (with a capital F). They should do, because all the old boy's protagonists certainly are. Instead, we go through Weymouth and the small town of Wool. I like the juxtaposition of life's essentials on this route, with Beer at one end and Wool at the other. There is also the village of Giddy Green, which sounds like it should be fun.

I can't say the same of my first impressions of Poole. It's one of those towns, not uncommon in this country, that consists of a handsome old part buried under a hideous new bit. We arrive in the new, which is basically a sprawling Arndale Centre with surrounding collateral damage, where I'm fortunate in being unable to find anywhere to stay. Eventually, in the old section down towards the quay, I find a backstreet pub with a perfectly serviceable room for £20 a night, breakfast included. They aren't actually serving food at night, but the off-duty Spanish chef has put a few extra things on the menu and the landlady wants to have a stab at cooking them, just in case he ever goes missing as the hungry Iberian mariners arrive. I'm not too proud to be a guinea pig. Also in the bar is a craggy Australian, an ex-soldier, from Rooty Hill in Sydney's far west. 'You won't have heard of it,' he says confidently.

I was able to tell him that, not only had I heard of it, I'd watched rugby league there. We pass an hour debating the scandalous state of the obstruction rule and complimenting the landlady on her unique take on tapas. It feels like the crossroads of the world. We're calling each other 'mate' – always bearing in mind that, whilst in the rest of the world that's a declaration of friendship, in Australia it means you've forgotten somebody's name.

There are those who will tell you that another major player on the English pub scene, the chatty young barmaid, is an extinct species. Not in Poole, she isn't. I can only describe this one as a South coast version of Tina from *Coronation Street*; bright, beautiful and effervescent, with a dash of attitude. Nothing remotely improper, I promise you, but we have a real good chat about the subjects that pre-occupy 19-year-old barmaids in Dorset, like rugby league, real ale, traditional folk music, coastal erosion and concessionary bus travel. It's only after an hour or so that I notice that the inside of both her forearms carry regularly-spaced scars, either from cuts or burns. I can't help but see it as evidence of self-harm; of some dark side to the psyche of this apparently happy individual with her life in front of her. I fervently hope as well that she doesn't get bludgeoned to death outside a builder's yard like Tina in *Corrie*.

All it needed was for the saloon doors to fly open and Poole's most famous resident – and patron saint of self-harm – to stagger in. The town is where that walking shipwreck, Paul Gascoigne, chooses to weigh anchor when he is between sanatoria.

SOMEWHERE between Poole and Bournemouth, the Jurassic Coast mutates into the Geriatric Coast. Even the residents refer to it as God's Waiting Room and, as a visitor, you can't help but notice that all the bus routes seem to go via the hospital. Beyond that is Christchurch and beyond that Lymington and the New Forest – a gap on the map and a complete mystery to me until this point.

Route 63

From Lymington, you not only get views of the Seven Sisters, you can even get a ferry to the Isle of Wight. One of my fellow passengers tells me triumphantly that he had been over there the previous weekend and that they accepted the free bus pass. I can't really justify a diversion, because, if I took one, I would have to call the book 'Ticket to Ryde,' which would not be a good thing. Instead, it's a change of bus in Lymington and a plunge into the Forest.

Not quite the density of trees I'd been led to expect. I'd half anticipated being issued with machetes to hack our way through the undergrowth. It isn't quite like that, although it does fulfil the main Route 63 criterion of being quite different from anywhere else in the country. The first pub I spot, for instance, is The Snakecatcher's Arms and they don't exactly grow on trees. There are also plenty of horses; in fact, in some of the quieter villages, there are horses grazing and sunning themselves in front gardens, but no people. It's eerily as though the horses have taken over, *Planet of the Apes*-style. The human beings are back in control by Southampton, after a transitional area around Totton, which, I have it on good authority, is ruled by Centaurs.

There are still massive ships, container and passenger, in the Western Docks, as well as the South Pier, a reminder of Southampton's former life as a fashionable seaside resort, soon effortlessly superceded by Brighton. Southampton's buses are scattered around a curiously dead part of the city centre, its bus station having been bulldozed long ago. This is almost always a mistake, denying the long-distance passenger a focus for his comings and goings. The best I can find is a slow bus to Portsmouth, where I plan to spend the night. In Fareham, about two-thirds of the way there, however, I have a rush of blood to the head and jump off, because it looks vaguely manageable and welcoming.

My feet have hardly touched the ground before I realise that I had seriously over-estimated Fareham. For one thing, there appeared to be nowhere to stay. The Tourist Information office, which couldn't wait to close – a pattern emerging here – could only suggest a pub which seemed to have the builders in, at an eye-watering £129 for a single, without breakfast. Eventually, from a dusty box-file that hadn't been opened for some time, they reluctantly produced the details of an out-of-town place which, at less than half that price, was still extortionate.

Fareham must have been a pleasant place once upon a time, but it has been ruined by a hideous flyover that separates it from its harbour. Having weighed up the town centre alternatives, I decide that I'll go to the harbour to watch England's World Cup match against Costa Rica. In an ideal world, I'd fulfil my contractual obligation to *The Independent* by watching it somewhere with a Costa Rican connection, but that proves surprisingly difficult. Costa Coffee doesn't count, I should add. Failing that, I go down an alleyway beside a supermarket, under the flyover and onto the harbour, where there is a pub with the singularly appropriate name – at World Cup time - of The Castle in the Air.

The reference is to Portchester Castle just across the water, which, in a certain sort of low-lying sea mist, used to give the illusion of hovering above the ground. There's too much in the way for that to happen now, but I'm obliged to my dining and match-watching companions for the explanation. I'm talking in particular to two chaps of about my age. One, originally from Burnley, is the local postman and thinks Fareham is the best place on earth. His mate has never lived anywhere else and describes it succinctly as 'a shit-hole,' ruined by planners and property developers.

I have, they congratulate me, found the only decent pub in Fareham, although the postman, who, I suspect, is not entirely a stranger to the occasional refreshing gill on his rounds, recommends a couple in the nearby village of Wallington. He's quite right about the pubs, so that makes a delightful late evening riverside stroll. Only the sandbags piled around the doorways give away the fact that it isn't always as restful and benign as this.

Back in the beer garden of my hotel, I reflect on just how much you can cram into an English summer's day. We all know that the English summer is not perfect; it is wet, cold and unreliable. But, when the weather, by some oversight, is set fair, the days go on forever. It's one of the drawbacks of warmer places of the world that, just as you're starting to enjoy them, it goes dark. On a good English day in late June, on the other hand, I've got up at my leisure, had my breakfast, walked across Poole, caught four buses, seen the New Forest and Southampton, explored Fareham on both sides of the flyover, watched England and Costa Rica with a big platter of fish, walked a couple of miles to a riverside village, come back for a nightcap at my hotel, written 600 words – and it's still light! So, two cheers for Farnham – and that's being generous – but three for the English summer's day.

All the same, when I get to Portsmouth the following morning, I realise I have made a mistake. Bigger towns and cities can be awkward, with bus stations miles away from anywhere to eat, drink or sleep. Not Pompey. The buses operate out of an interchange in an area curiously called The Hard and that's exactly the part of Portsmouth where you'd choose to be, next to the historic ships, the old sailors' pubs and, I would guess, the cheap hotels. It would also have been the most westerly claim on the name of Charles Dickens, who lived here for his first six months, but wrote nothing of note in that time. Oh well, I'll have a look next time.

The road leads through Havant to the beautiful little cathedral city of Chichester, past Bognor Regis – subject of King George V's most memorable quote: 'Bugger Bognor' – Arundel, a contender for the title of England's most idyllic cricket ground, and Littlehampton, a name surely made up by the people who brought us the most risqué of seaside postcards, the ones kept at the top of the wire rack. Then it's along the front, through Worthing, Shoreham, Portslade and Hove, by which time the remains of one of Brighton's piers are in view and we know we have arrived in Sin City.

BRIGHTON's beach is a disgrace, a national embarrassment. In fact, they've got a nerve calling it a beach at all; it's just a heap of stones.

Mind you, my view could be jaundiced by my first visit as – I'm telling the truth here – an eight-year-old choirboy. I lost the rest of the party as effortlessly as I lost the right key when singing on a Sunday and, as it all looked the same, couldn't find them. Eventually, they found me running up and down the slopes of rounded stones in increasing agitation which, musically at least, can only have been a disappointment to them.

The most characteristic sight in Brighton now is of crowds of teenaged trippers from France, Italy or wherever looking over the edge of the promenade and saying to each other, in their various tongues: 'This is it, Brighton beach? This heap of stones?'

That is not to say that it is devoid of interest. There

are, for instance, the remains of Volk's Electric Railway, which is the successor to one of the wackier transport concepts of the 19th century, his Seashore Electric Railway, which was essentially a raised platform on rails which ran along the sands allegedly revealed at low tide, towards Rottingdean. It lasted five years, from 1896 to 1901.

There are now people living on the beach, at least on a part-time basis, and there is a nudist section. There is more than that going on. In September 2014, the *Daily Mail* reported that a couple had been spotted having sex on the beach 'in broad daylight'. Apparently, quite a few people gathered around to watch and one attempted to join in. A less impressed observer called it an orgy worthy of the decline and fall of Rome. If I'd had a landmark like that to refer to, though, I never would have got lost on the choir day trip. Right by the Punch 'n' Judy, left by the shagging couple and you're there.

This all tallies quite neatly with the national perception of Brighton, except that the town's current reputation would call for at least one same-sex couple to be taking their pleasure on the pebbles. Brighton rejoices in its unofficial title as the Gay Capital of Europe and it would be unnatural for exhibitionists of that persuasion to be left out. Brighton has gone from being the spiritual home of the dirty weekend and of stage-managed adultery for divorce purposes to become England's Gay Central. For Sodom and Gomorrah read Brighton and Hove.

One consequence of that demographic is that there is disposable income aplenty. Brighton has around 400 restaurants, more than anywhere outside London; hungry business, being gay.

With time to kill, I spend an hour or two dozing in the park behind the Royal Pavilion, arguably the most extravagant and eccentric building of the whole trip, with its array of preposterous domes and minarets. One small problem is that the seagulls have chosen this as their eaterie of choice and they swoop on anything unattended.

I'm looking for somewhere genuinely unusual for a snack and I think I've found it in the shape of the Blue Man Tuareg Café. I'm fairly confident that this is Brighton's only Tuareg Café and I have mint tea and olives, whilst being serenaded by a couple from Aireys Inlet on the Great Ocean Road near Melbourne. It's that sort of city.

It's now getting close to the appointed hour for my rendezvous with my mate, Nigel, one of the thousands who lives in Brighton and commutes to work in London. He has a bit of a Jekyll and Hyde thing going on. By day, a mild-mannered newspaper executive; after the sun dips behind the West Pier, a beer monster. It's Mr Hyde that I'm expecting, but when I get to The Evening Star I'm still too early and I know from experience that the last thing you want to do on a session with Nige is to start off a couple of pints ahead.

I repair instead to an arty little café across the street, with wooden crates doubling as tables and chairs on the pavement. I buy a baguette – feta cheese, hummus and rocket, since you ask – but, as I'm returning to my crate, the biggest seagull you've ever seen pounces and snatches away my sandwich in its cruel and greedy beak. Quick as a flash, the girl in the café runs out, brush in hand, and wallops him so that he drops his prize before he gets properly airborne. She dusts off the still-wrapped baguette and returns it to me, as though this happens every day. It probably does.

The Evening Star, not far from Brighton station, is everything it's cracked up to be. For one thing it's the brewery tap for Dark Star beers, which I personally rate as the best in the country. This will be close to heresy in the eyes of a lot of northern beer-drinkers. With so much excellent ale on the doorstep, how can I prefer something originating from Brighton, of all places, and now brewed a few miles inland at the bucolic-sounding Partridge Green? It's a clear case of regional treachery. I can only refer you to the evidence of my taste buds. Everything I've ever had from them has been superb – with a trademark thump of fresh hops – although perhaps not quite as superb as it is here, on its home turf. Nige is on fine form as well, regaling me with the progress of the rugby league team he helps to run, the Sussex Merlins.

There is no getting away from the fact that this is Brighton, however. Take this conversation between two apparent strangers in the gents', for instance.

'I must compliment you,' says one flamboyant character to another, 'on your splendidly deep voice.'

'On the contrary,' says that other fellow, 'I was just thinking what a wonderfully deep voice you have.'

'Hang on a minute,' I wanted to shout, like Brian Blessed again. 'I've got a deeper voice than either of you and I don't go around bragging about it.' But, somewhere in the back of my head, a quiet little voice said: 'Leave it, Dave. Say nothing.' And, for once, I listened.

Several pubs and a comatose sleep later, I'm lurching out of Nige's flat in Hove. The man himself is long gone – testimony to his iron constitution – but he has left me a sketch map of my route to the bus, including, without irony, a thoroughfare called Dykes Road.

● *Since I trod those streets, the newly elected Conservative government has announced that it is scrapping the body set up to study the phenomenon of urban seagulls. In fact, that seems to be the only saving they have specifically identified. Where have these people been? Have they never been to the cinema? Have they never risked life and limb with an unprotected baguette in Brighton?*

Prostrate with Dismal

BRIGHTON has hit upon an innovative way of making bus travel even more confusing than it is everywhere else. Where your bus stops can depend on the time of day. By the time I unravel this unusual system, I'm down by the Palace Pier, waiting for the number 12 to Eastbourne.

Visitors to Brighton once used to have their choice of two piers, but the West Pier is closed and derelict. It's part of a national decline. The National Pier Society lists 48 that are still in usable condition in England. Blackpool is the only resort with three, but those with two make up an interesting list: Great Yarmouth, Lowestoft, Southsea, Weston-super-Mare and Weymouth. Suffice to say that dual-pier ownership is no guarantee of glamour and sophistication.

The NPS also lists 34 'lost' English piers and its website is full of items about piers under threat, piers closing and, just occasionally, piers re-opening. They are, as we see all too clearly on this stretch of the English coast, almost by definition, terribly vulnerable structures. With little appetite to repair the casualties, you can just about imagine the time when one of their number is the last pier standing. At the time of writing, the company which owns the South and Central Piers in Blackpool, plus one of Wales' best in Llandudno, had put all three up for sale.

Somewhere between the eastward sprawl of Brighton and the rise of the South Downs, there is the village of Rottingdean. This is a rather special place, not just because it was once home to Rudyard Kipling. The superstar scribe lived there for five years around the turn of the 19th century, before settling inland at Burwash. One reason he opted for a more remote location is that trippers used to come from London to stare over his fence at him. Contrast that with his reputation for much of the 20th century, when he went so far out of fashion with academics that he was barely visible. Part of his problem was that he was the Poet of Empire and there was little call for that. He never lost his appeal to the ordinary reader, however. Such is the breadth and sheer quantity of his output that there must be something there that anyone can use, even if it's only *If*.

Rather less well-known is that Rottingdean is home to the Copper Family, generations of traditional singers who have had a major influence on the revival of English folk music. The Coppers I came across were Ron, the landlord of the Queen Victoria pub – still there on the main square of the village, a couple of hundred yards from the sea – and his erudite cousin, Bob. Apart from his peerless singing of English country songs, Bob loved another genre of music and left behind recordings which have recently been released on a CD entitled *Prostrate with Dismal: Bob Copper Sings the Blues*. Prostrate with Dismal? That was how Bob's grandfather, Jim, said the growing urbanisation of Rottingdean and the South Downs in general made him feel when he was interviewed by the BBC in 1951, but it still looks pretty good to me.

At Newhaven, a few people get on who have obviously got off the ferry from Dieppe, one of the lesser-known cross-Channel routes. From there, the road climbs to one of the most famous – or infamous – spots on the whole of the South Coast.

Beachy Head is, by some distance, Britain's favourite suicide venue. Indeed, it is outranked globally by only the Golden Gate Bridge in San Francisco and some particularly gloomy woods in Japan. If you really are prostrate with dismal, it is the place to be – and only a 20 mile bus ride from Rottingdean. Beachy Head is a mere 162 metres high, but, as they say around these parts, it's only the last few that kill you. There's a big notice from the Samaritans on the clifftop and another in the nearest pub, urging you not to do anything silly. 'And they keep a bit of an eye on you if you book a single,' says the man sitting next to me.

After that, the sight, around the next corner, of Eastbourne, is distinctly uplifting. From above, it looks like a miniature, idealised Brighton. In fact, much of the film of Graham Greene's novel *Brighton Rock* was shot in Eastbourne, because it looked more the part, more like Brighton than Brighton did. It certainly had a magnificent pier. I say 'had' because, in the few weeks between visiting and writing, a section of it burnt down, probably deliberately, leaving the National Pier Society prostrate with dismal.

By contrast, you get the distinct impression that no-one would care very much if the whole of Hastings was to burn down. Its problems could be said to date back to *1066 and All That*, when it was wrongly fingered as the scene of the great disaster of English history. On 14 October, the Normans landed at Pevensey, Harold took one in the eye for the team – at least according to the Bayeux Tapestry – and William the Bastard became William the Conquerer. If you take a strictly Anglo-Saxon view of history, it was the day everything started to go wrong. It did so a good five miles from Hastings, close to the village of Battle. Despite that, we have persisted for the last thousand years or so in calling it the Battle of Hastings. What are we to call it, though? The Battle of Pevensey? The Battle of Battle? Kipling doesn't have an answer to that one, but he is the man to consult about the long-term significance of the Norman victory, because no-one writes as eloquently as he about England's ability to absorb wave after wave of invaders and in-comers.

Modern-day Hastings gets a terrible press, of the Squalor-on-Sea type that also attaches itself to Blackpool and Morecambe. It undeniably has a big drug problem and there are parts of the town which are badly run-down. I'd still rather be down-and-out there than in plenty of inland dumping grounds I can think of. There is plenty of fun to be had on the South Coast, it seems to me, beating each other with the sticks that everyone in Brighton is gay, everyone in Eastbourne is ancient and everyone in Hastings is on drugs and benefits. If there is any reader out there who qualifies on all three counts, you really deserve your bus pass, but for heaven's sake take it a bit easy.

Hastings was one of the Cinque Ports, which had a special trading relationship with the continent from the Middle Ages onward. Membership of the elite group is now of limited value to two of the five originals, as New Romney and Sandwich are no longer on the coast. Hastings has at least avoided that indignity, but, as you climb out of town, there is a gable-end the size of a paramilitary mural in Belfast, reading: 'Welcome to Ore Village.' You can almost hear the unwritten parentheses: 'Nothing to do With That Place Down the Hill.' Even though they haven't yet learned to spell 'our.'

Kent: Deal or no Deal

WHEN they christened Kent the Garden of England, it is doubtful whether they had in mind Derek Jarman's plot at Dungeness. If there's one thing wrong with the bus route in these parts, at least with the one I'm on – it is that it doesn't take a detour to this weirdest of locations. Here, on the flat shingle in the shadow of the nuclear power station, the artist and film-maker somehow created a spectacular garden, full of plants that not only survived the unpromising environment, but thrived in it.

The trade-off is that we do go to Lydd, on the edge of Denge Marsh, a place so desolate that it makes Dungeness look like the Hanging Gardens of Babylon and the Amazon Rainforest rolled into one. Lydd isn't unspoilt wilderness – far from it – but it feels like part of the country that has quietly curled up and died. 'Ready for the quiet life?' asks a poster at one of the apparently deserted caravan parks. Possibly, but not completely silent, thank you very much.

The only thing stirring this afternoon is the one-time Lydd Airport, which now parades its wares as a confidence trick called London-Ashford. It isn't anywhere near London, it isn't anywhere near Ashford; it isn't even all that close to Lydd. It does fly the short hop to Le Touquet, though, and to Verona. I pity anyone from either of those places who flies into Lydd thinking that London exists there as anything more than a hazy rumour.

By comparison, Dymchurch and Hythe, with their narrow gauge railway running along the sea front, are visions of loveliness and Folkestone seems to go forever. I had intended to go all the way to Ramsgate, but I was starting to recognise the first tell-tale signs of being bussed-out; numb bum, a worse twitch than usual and a lack of concentration that makes the outside world go past in a blur.

Besides, Dover – a place I'd been through dozens of times, but never stayed and never heard anyone say a good word about – is looking surprisingly seductive. Its bus station, uniquely on my travels, is in a green, leafy park. And what would I be missing? Another Kentish seaside town with a castle and a rocky beach. Big Deal....

Route 63

I was right about Dover. The area where I disembark is full of big 19th century houses, turned into guest houses. I book into one with a strong Churchillian theme and I'm assigned the Chartwell Room, which even has a balcony; well, it has a fire escape where you can sit out and that's enough to put me in a good mood.

Across the road is Dover's oldest pub, the Black Horse, which has an unusual approach to interior decoration. The walls and ceilings are covered with signatures of people, old and young, from all over the world, who have swum the English Channel. It seems an awful lot of swimmers to me, which sparks a typical bar-room debate over whether or not everyone who has left their autograph has actually braved the 20 miles to Cap Gris Nez. The killer argument: 'Well, my name's up there,' says one of the regulars, 'and I've never swum the bleedin' thing.'

Dover doesn't make a big thing of its beach, despite Matthew Arnold's 'Dover Beach' – one of the better-known short poems in the English language.

> The sea is calm tonight
> The tide is full, the moon lies fair.

It's actually a very pleasant place to be. There's a water-sports centre with a restaurant and a balcony overlooking the sea. It also looks out past the young kayakers, through the gap between sea walls to what must be France on the horizon. It's a trick of the lowering sun that, every time you look at it, France seems a little closer and I dare say that's sometimes the way you feel if you live there and follow events in Calais.

Mine host at the guest house is a good example. Originally from London, he fell in love with Dover and has lived there for the last 40 years. It brings out the patriot in him. When he had finished interrogating me, I watched and listened entranced over breakfast to see just how far he would go with subtly baiting two middle-aged Germans who were embarking on a drive around England.

'You like England, don't you?' he says, not quite adding, because he doesn't have to: 'Well, you can't have it.'

The other guest at breakfast is a solemn Russian youth in his late teens. 'His dad's an oligarch,' he says in a loud whisper. 'Left him here for the summer. Seems happy enough.'

Back in the park the following morning, there are plenty of buses to Canterbury, but having got there, they seem to go around it, rather than into it. Eventually, I find one to Faversham, a town I decided I liked before I got there. For one thing, it's close to the centre of the hop-growing area of Kent; for another, it's home to what claims to be the oldest brewery in the country. There are plenty of characterful Shepherd Neame pubs on the market square and nearby streets, all serving their distinctive, heavily-hopped beers. And so onto another bus to Sittingbourne, a place about which I can remember absolutely nothing to tell you.

We're closing in now on the Medway towns, a blanket term to cover a number of very different places running into each other. There's down-at-heel Gillingham, aspirational and historic Rochester, and Chatham, former site of the Royal Dockyard, where Dickens' father took his family when he landed a job there. At Chatham Waterfront bus station, there are connections for exotic-sounding destinations, like Allhallows and Hoo, the former of which sounds spooky, the latter merely unfinished, and the Isle of Grain.

It's a thoroughly obscure backwater, but it was briefly in the news later in the summer when Grain was rejected as a possible site for the new London airport – well, it's closer than Lydd – despite the support of the city's mayor; hence its new alternative name – Boris Island. There are no buses to London, though; the best they can suggest at the ultra-modern bus station, which is actually reminiscent of a small airport, if not a Boris Island sized one, is to get one to Bluewater and pick up a connection there.

At the mention of Bluewater my blood runs cold. I know what it is; it's an out-of-town shopping centre, places that give me the heebie-jeebies even more acutely than High Street shops. It's a place where men go in and never come out again. I have visions of being stranded there, among its 300 stores and 60 eating places, and having to be rescued by the SAS. Imagine my relief, therefore, when the road curves down a feeder road towards a bus terminus full of gleaming red London Transport double-deckers. There surely must be one going my way. Sure enough, there's one for Lewisham, from where I can get to Euston to meet my son. I've allowed about five hours for this simple little journey. What can possibly go wrong?

No sooner do we start, though, than we stop. It goes on for miles and hours, this staccato rhythm of stop, go, stop, stop, go. Inevitably, this leads to the phenomenon known as bunching. I think I promised you a scientific explanation of this earlier on, so here goes, with thanks to BBC Radio 4, which devoted most of a programme to this vexed question not long ago.

When vehicles travelling at different speeds occupy the same stretch of road, the tendency will be for those moving at a similar speed to group together. Hence the irritation of three buses arriving at the same time; they didn't start off that way, but there's this inexorable force pulling them together. Without amending the laws of mathematics, there isn't a great deal that can be done about it. Sorry to be the bearer of bad tidings.

I thought that was the end of the matter, but bus guru Cudbertson says that it's not quite right.

Over to him then.

'Let's imagine we are waiting on a busy road with a bus due every five minutes. Further back an unexpected delay has occurred which affects three buses in succession but to different degrees. In getting late to our stop it is inevitable that the first bus will pick up more passengers than if it were on time, meaning more time needed for people to board and more time for those people to alight. Meanwhile the second bus, though delayed, has consequently fewer passengers waiting at stops, so it makes better than expected progress in making good its lost time. By now the third, which was only marginally affected by the original problem, also has fewer to pick up and catches the first two. Bingo! Three together.'

I don't know whether I'm dazzled by a flash of insight, or merely blinded by science.

Our bus, the one in front of it and the one behind it move in convoy, very slowly, through a lot of very similar places. Plumstead sticks in my mind for some reason, probably only because I like the name. It slowly becomes apparent, however, that, if I stay on the bus battling its way through the traffic, all the way to the end of the line, I'm not going to get to Euston in time.

YOU can find a red bus going your way just about anywhere in London and its surrounds. The trouble is that, by the time you get there, you might well have forgotten why you wanted to go there in the first place. That's certainly the case with this journey. As time ticks on and we crawl between stops, I start to look for somewhere to jump off. Then I spot the Woolwich Arsenal DLR station and think 'I've heard of that.' It's actually the furthest outpost of the DLR – Docklands Light Railway – which is London's most futuristic transport option. It doesn't even have drivers, for heaven's sake! It will whisk me to Euston, via Bank, in no time. It's not until I read up about it afterwards that I realise that, in Woolwich, I've made an inspired choice. That's London for you; love it or hate it, but you can be dropped almost anywhere at random and find that it has a few tales to tell.

That is resoundingly true of Woolwich. It has always been one of the most important crossing points on the Thames and still offers the choice of the Woolwich Free Ferry and a foot tunnel. I used to have a girlfriend in Charlton and my preferred means of arrival was aboard the ferry from the imaginatively-named North Woolwich. Just a hint there of the intrepid mariner, back from the Seven Seas, which always went down well. Failing that, it was a walk through the tunnel, which smelt of piss and mud.

Just downstream is Gallions Reach, scene of the Thames' worst disaster, in 1878 when a pleasure steamer called the Princess Alice was sliced in two by a collier brig and 600 people were drowned in a matter of minutes. Going a little upstream, you soon come to the Thames Barrier, built to protect the city from the river's more wilful moods and largely successful at doing so.

On dry land, the last London tram started its final journey in Woolwich in 1952. In 1974, McDonald's opened their first English branch in Woolwich, apparently because they considered it to be typical of the country as a whole. Had they never heard of the Man on the Clapham Omnibus?

There is nothing typical about some of the things that have happened to Woolwich since. In 1974, the King's Arms pub was bombed by the Provisional IRA, killing two. Woolwich was also caught up in the London Riots of 2011, with a number of businesses burnt out. This was down-page news compared with the horror of the death of the soldier, Lee Rigby, who was butchered by two Islamic extremists close to Woolwich Barracks. That's Woolwich for you; nothing much ever happens.

For many people, the name of the place will always have a football resonance. The club that became Arsenal began life as Woolwich Arsenal, playing at the Manor Ground in Plumstead. They were effectively a works team attached to the Royal Arsenal, suppliers of armaments to the world, but they became the first southern team to join the northern-dominated Football League. In 1913, they moved to Highbury in North London and a year later dropped the Woolwich from their name.

Relocating in this way is unusual in English football, but West Ham will attempt it when they move into the Olympic Stadium in Stratford. Arsenal, meanwhile, have moved a second time, but only about 500 yards down the road to the Emirates Stadium, whilst Woolwich is Charlton Athletic territory. And Woolwich – did I mention the building society? – is where I call it quits for this leg of the journey.

Diversion: That London

I HAVE to admit that I had planned to bypass London completely, or, at the most, sneak in and out of it under the cover of darkness. I was under the impression that I could ignore it, the way that I was already committed to cold-shoulder Birmingham. The difference is that, whilst the horrors of Brum – and particularly the Seven Circles of Hell radiating from New Street Station – are not really on my route, the horrors of London undeniably are.

It was my son Sam, now happily resident in Bethnal Green, who talked me out of my reluctance and persuaded me that I couldn't de-materialise in Woolwich and re-appear, as if by magic, in Stratford. England, after all, is at least as centralised as any other country in the world, with the possible exception of France, and, ultimately, all roads and all bus routes lead to That London, with its scary crowds and scarier prices.

My route through my missing bit of London, however, is meant to begin by going underwater. There are at least 26 tunnels under the Thames – the relevant authorities are rather vague on exact numbers – but the one we are interested in goes the 504 metres from Woolwich to North Woolwich. Or it does when it's open; problems with leakage saw it closed for over a year early in this decade. The good news now is that not only can you cross to the other side without swimming, you can also get a mobile phone signal. It still smells of piss, though.

Getting there from Bethnal Green involves catching the DLR from Stratford, which is like an excursion into a different century. At one stage, it crosses paths with the wackiest of all London's public transport options, the Emirates Air Line, strung overhead like a child's drawing for a school project on solving the city's transport problems. There is also an unusual view of the Thames Barrier, which, from this angle, looks like a line of abandoned off-cuts from the Sydney Opera House or a giant's stepping stones.

The tunnel and the ferry both involve walking through the shopping centre, past two huge churches –

previously cinemas, by the look of them – glaring at each other across a roundabout, before getting to Woolwich Pier, another of the destinations that sets me humming, because Ewan MacColl's 'Sweet Thames Flow Softly' starts with the line: 'I met my love at Woolwich Pier, beneath the big crane standing.'

There are still cranes at work there, but their role now is not loading and unloading cargo, but redeveloping the waterfront. The trouble is that following the numerous signposts for the tunnel around the building site delivers you not at the tunnel, but at the ferry. It really doesn't matter, because the title of the Woolwich Free Ferry includes that vital F-word – and I don't mean Ferry. I mean Free. Using it to cross the Thames is therefore well within the guidelines for this little adventure. Passengers are few in number, but there is a long queue of pissed-off looking lorry drivers at the southern terminus, waiting to take their vehicles across. I take the option of a best of both worlds venture into the tunnel from the north side. There is nobody else to read the notice forbidding, amongst other things, Littering, Loitering and Busking. Anyone who spends lonely hours picking out a tune down there deserves some loose change, surely. And I bet the acoustics are sensational.

On the otherwise deserted north bank, there is a bus waiting, with its driver enjoying a brew and checking whether *The Sun* really has done away with its Page 3 girls. When you think of some of the roaring racetracks and stationary snarl-ups he could be having to negotiate, this looks suspiciously like the cushiest billet at the depot. 'Oh no,' they must groan. 'Not the 473 again. What have I done to deserve this?' Even when we get going – just me and him, nobody else until we get to the Chinese supermarket – he still seems to have London Transport's most relaxing job. We breeze in and out of London City Airport, cruise through Plaistow, where the Black Lion pub has something that is a lot less common than it used to be – a seafood stall in its car park. It almost has me scrambling down the steps to investigate, although I know that by seafood they mean mainly cockles and whelks in vinegar. There are also still pie and mash shops around these parts, if you know where to look, some of them serving that most acquired of tastes, jellied eels.

Enough of this gastro-porn; we glide into Stratford and I'm officially back on track.

The double-decker bus has been an integral part of life and death for Londoners ever since engines replaced horses. The singer, Jez Lowe, commissioned to write an upbeat song about the First World War for a commemorative project, produced one called 'The Wrong Bus,' about passengers getting on board in the heart of the capital and finishing up on the Somme. There is a factual basis behind this apparently fanciful idea, because British soldiers really were delivered to the front in London double-deckers shipped across to Belgium for that purpose.

There is a jaw-dropping Pathé newsreel film clip of the Tommies waving cheerfully from the upper deck on what, for many of them, was a one-way trip requiring only a single ticket. They looked for all the world as though they were off on their holidays. Actually, nearly nine out of ten Britons who fought in the Great War returned home to tell the tale. I suspect that the odds were quite a bit worse for the infantrymen arriving at the trenches on the buses.

It's all as bizarre a juxtaposition as the French sending re-inforcements to the front during the First Battle of the Marne in a fleet of 600 Parisian taxi cabs. Imagine trying to get one to the Gare du Nord that day; and trust the French to take their creature comforts with them.

I thought the London Transport Museum would know more about the bus connection. By an extraordinary piece of good luck, however, the Saturday I had to be in London co-incided with the museum getting what it billed as its 'Battle Bus' out for a spin at its depot in Acton. I say good luck; I'm not entirely certain that Sam, whom I was visiting, really wanted to spend his Saturday morning off charging across London to see an old bus, even the B-type numbered B2737, but he humoured me.

Battle Bus has become a convenient short-hand for the vehicles in which political leaders – British or American – career around marginal constituencies during election campaigns. But any battling they see is of the purely figurative variety – unless John Prescott is involved, of course – and, by any definition, they are coaches rather than buses.

We are concerned here with the other meaning – the genuine service buses that went to war. London Transport has one, lovingly restored to the way it looked in 1914. The gleaming red and cream livery of the London General Omnibus Company was a bit of a giveaway for German snipers, so it is replaced by a paint job the colour of mud or sodden khaki uniforms, with boarded-up windows on the lower deck and an open upper deck for those intent on taking in the view. There are 13 of us privileged to be seeing this historic vehicle and some of the others are in a state of what I can only describe as Bus Ecstasy.

'You know what?' says Sam. 'We're the least nerdy people here.' And, as he points out, it's not often he's been able to say that.

One of the distinguishing features of the bus buff – although it probably applies to other forms of transport as well – is that he shares in a thread of bus humour that is incomprehensible to outsiders.

Our guides, or one of the party of 13, will say something gnomic about the tyres or the engine and the rest will chuckle appreciatively. Oh well, I suppose it keeps them off the streets. I thought one or two were going to faint with pleasure when it was confirmed that the Battle Bus was going to be brought out of the aircraft hangar-sized depot building to give us a ride. It is, in all honesty, a pretty short ride and rather a jerky one. On the positive side, at least the Germans aren't shelling us. Some of us are in such a state of bliss that we wouldn't notice if they were.

There are some other good yarns at the London Transport Museum at Covent Garden, which there should be when it costs £13.50 for a year's admission.

'Can't I just pay to come in once?' I ask.

'Of course you can. That'll be £13.50.'

Anxious to get value for my money, I think I might have to spend my summer holidays here, probably in one of the Tube carriages. On this visit, I home in on the story of Joseph Clough, a Jamaican who became London's first black bus driver in 1908. A racist supervisor managed to get him suspended for a time on a trumped-up charge of speeding. If there isn't an Andrew Lloyd Webber musical in that, I don't know where one is.

Public Transport in London has been the arena for a number of struggles for equality. The 'Colour Bar Strike' in 1957 saw white railwaymen at King's Cross refuse to work with black recruits. I remember a particularly heated political discussion on my journalists' training course when I advanced this as evidence that not absolutely every strike could be justified politically. The fully paid-up Marxists on the course were having none of it. It didn't fit, so it can't have happened. The Workers Cannot be Wrong. MacColl, a hard-line Marxist himself, wrote the song, or rather he wrote the tune to a poem by a railwayman, Charlie Mayo, so he presumably knew better. There was also resistance to the prospect of female Tube drivers; one Hannah Dadds became the first in 1978. Discriminatory barriers were not unique to London, either. There was a boycott of buses in Bristol in the early-sixties, in protest at the operators' shameful but long-established policy of not recruiting from ethnic minorities.

That situation could not be more different in the part of London I have in my sights next. For just once in my life, I want to be the Man on the Clapham Omnibus. But which Clapham?

Taking a Tube map as my guide, I have a choice of Clapham Junction, Clapham North, Clapham Common and Clapham South. If I prefer the overground, there is the option of Clapham High Street. I vote for none of the above, however, plumping instead for a remote region of Clapham without a station to its name – Clapham Park.

There is what looks like an interesting route to it from Stratford, involving just one change. It also takes me through the Bethnal Green that my son now calls home.

I've already seen enough of the area to recognise that it has the one great advantage of living in London – its almost infinite variety. Take our little tour the previous evening; sandwiched in between two pubs brewing their own 'craft' beers, we have our tea at a Korean café between Cambridge Heath and Bethnal Green. Like many small businesses in this part of London, it is crammed into a railway arch. In this case, available space is divided between the restaurant and a unisex Korean hairdressers. When the snipping ends for the day at around 8.00pm, the salon is rearranged with a couple of tables pulled out and becomes part of the café. So, if your food isn't hot enough, you could, in theory, warm it up under a hair-dryer.

Not that this should be necessary; the food is hot in both the sense of spice and of temperature. If I'd come in 15 minutes earlier, I could have had a haircut as well. Among its other eccentricities, it promises to do its work in a quarter of an hour; if it takes longer, you pay less, on a sliding scale. It's a system that could catch on.

A rather different expression of the diversity of the area comes along a couple of weeks later when three 15 and 16-year-old girls from Bethnal Green Academy bunk off school, not to hang around the precinct and smoke illicit cigs in the traditional manner, but to fly to Turkey, cross into Syria and join up with the murderous nutters of Islamic State.

The route of the bus goes past Liverpool Street and through the fiscal canyons of the City of London, from which it emerges near London Bridge, which is a replacement for the one famously sold to the Yanks of Lake Havasu City in Arizona, where they supposedly thought they were getting Tower Bridge as a tourist attraction, rather than the unremarkable structure that used to carry the city's name and the A3 across the river. It's a temptingly good story, hinging as it does on American gullibility, but unfortunately it does not seem to be true. At least, both buyer and seller denied it; but then, for their different reasons, they would, wouldn't they? The terminus is at the next bridge but one upstream, Blackfriars, where I initially manage to resist the temptation of a sneaky pint at the wonderfully ornate art nouveau pub of the same name, or rather the Black Friar, if you insist on being a stickler. It was once saved from demolition by a campaign led by Sir John Betjeman. I call in on the way back instead and I pay for the privilege, to the tune of £4.40. That London, it gets you every time; if I doesn't get you on the way in, it gets you on the way out.

Just around the corner there is a number 45, not at a

bus stop, but the driver lets me on anyway. Considering the stressful nature of their jobs, I'm finding London bus drivers a surprisingly relaxed lot. Ours takes us over Blackfriars Bridge, through Southwark and onwards to one of London's most mysterious locations, the Elephant and Castle.

It's basically a massive roundabout, with a central island that is so built-up it seems to be straining to spill out onto the roads that surround it. Its name has always held a fascination; the short explanation is that it was called after the coaching inn that stood on the site, but why was that called the Elephant and Castle? Well, you can forget the fanciful tale of a Spanish princess known as the Infanta of Castille. But does the rather dull explanation that it was lifted from the coat of arms of the cutlers, who were active hereabouts, sound any more convincing? The elephant was supposedly a reference to the ivory, from which the fanciest handles were made. I've heard the elephant and castle on Bolton's coat of arms attributed to the Indian connection, because that was where the raw cotton for Lancashire's mills came from. The truth is that, as even Stephen Fry sometimes has to admit, nobody knows.

One claim I don't have any trouble believing is that Elephant and Castle is the most dangerous roundabout in the country for cyclists. Mind you, the whole of London looks lethal to me for anyone on two wheels. Sam's girlfriend had been knocked off her bike a couple of weeks earlier and maybe it was the lingering concussion that persuaded her that what she really wanted to do with her Saturday night was watch Bolton play Liverpool with us in a pub in Camden Town.

Back on the number 45, it's next stop Camberwell Green, which looks surprisingly urban compared with the way I remember it from children's television. (Note: there might be some confusion here with *Camberwick Green*). The real attraction of this route, though, is that it goes straight through an area whose name everybody knows.

Brixton was as average as Clapham until the arrival of the Empire Windrush in 1948. The former German cruise ship, acquired as part of post-War reparations, brought around 500 passengers from Jamaica, including several stowaways and the island's three leading calypso singers. From their temporary accommodation when they landed, the nearest Labour Exchange at which to start looking for work was on Coldharbour Lane. The Brixton connection was established. There is now a Windrush Square and, if it's not quite spawned an ancestral nostalgia industry, like tracing your arrival in America on the Mayflower or in Australia on the First Fleet, there will still be plenty in the area who can make that link.

Brixton also has an Electric Avenue, as immortalized by the Eddy Grant hit. I suppose I would have assumed that it was a mythical address, dreamed up to sound catchy and exciting; but no, it's perfectly real and so called only for the rather mundane reason that it was one of the first streets in the country to be lit by electric lights.

Rather a lot has happened in Brixton since the Windrush dropped anchor in Tilbury docks. There were already bigger Caribbean populations in Liverpool, Bristol and Cardiff, for instance, but Brixton was on its way to becoming synonymous with West Indian life in Britain. It was part of the national fascination with 'the other'. Brixton did not represent assimilation; it stood for the exotic and the edgy – drugs, guns and gangs. One particularly vicious and notorious gang put a Brixton mobster in overall charge. But enough of John Major, a man so grey that he seemed to embody both black and white and make even running away with the circus seem conformist. There were riots in 1981, 1985 and 1995. White folks still went there, notably for the market and the music venues, but there was always a feeling that you were entering The Badlands and that you might be doing so at your own risk.

Everyone tells me that Brixton has changed; from the top deck of the Clapham Omnibus you can get a glimpse. From there, it looks a very average suburb, with a mixture of races and socio-economic groups. It certainly looks nothing like a ghetto. In London and other British cities, there is a process called gentrification, whereby previously neglected parts of the metropolis become fashionable and sought after. This has clearly happened to parts of Brixton, but nobody uses the word in a positive way. If they want to convey the idea of an area moving up-market, the favoured term is regeneration. You pay your mortgage and you take your choice. Perhaps it should be called regentrification, to cover both bases. I've no doubt some bad stuff still happens around there, as it does in the City of London, but the mood this Friday afternoon is about as threatening as in *Camberwick Green*.

The only time I hear a voice raised is when a passenger bewails the fact that he has to meet his daughter from school and, due to the slow progress of the number 45, he is going to be late. The driver is as patient as others I came across in London, explaining that he has little control over these matters.

The pub at the top of Brixton Hill admittedly has drug warnings writ a little larger than at the average Wetherspoons, but otherwise you could be anywhere in London. As for Clapham Park, it barely seems to exist at all, except as a bus destination. There is certainly no park that I can find, although in the *A to Z* it looks as though there could have been an extension of Clapham Common somewhere around. The Common has its own brand of notoriety, as one of the traditional spots where MPs with more varied sex lives than their constituents imagine are caught with their trousers down, as it were.

Brixton has its own little piece of London bus history. Think of a London bus and the chances are that what will spring to mind will be the classic double-decker Routemaster – the ones with the stairs at the back and the open platform that you can hop and off. There is a good deal of nostalgia for the old workhorse of the London streets. It has its own fan club and there have been frequent calls for the Routemaster, or something like it, to be re-introduced. The one-time Mayor of London, Ken Livingstone, however, took the view that they were far too dangerous, with a dozen deaths a year attributable to falls from the platform. An even more nailed on reason why they never seemed likely to return – except as novelties for the tourists at home or abroad – is that they only work with conductors on board and nobody was going to re-introduce them any time soon.

But here's a surprise. The new Routemaster 600 (or BorisMaster, as it might come to be called) is to be introduced on busy routes. During peak hours, they will carry conductors and have the 'hop on, hop off' platform. If no conductor is on board, the open back entrance is closed off. So the 129 bus that inched through massive crowds and turned right into Brixton Garage at the end of its route in 2005 on a ceremonial last journey is not doomed to remain the last Routemaster in regular service.

There was The Who's 'Magic Bus', not to mention the Knight Bus in the *Harry Potter* series. This was a triple-decker, which had the handy ability to shrink in width to squeeze through the tightest of traffic or the narrowest of alleys. The conventional night bus network, which is now extensive, is famous for eccentric and even alarming behaviour. There are now failed asylum seekers who just about live on them, or at least spend all night on them. You can't do that for free on a bus pass, though.

Buses rumble into your awareness all the time in London, sometimes in the strangest of circumstances. That same weekend, for instance, I'm sitting with Sam and his mate Jimmy outside a pub in Broadway Market. We are approached by a middle-aged black man, who says: 'Excuse me gentlemen, may I ask you something? What is your opinion of rising damp?'

'Well,' I tell him, 'none of us are experts, but I understand it can make a right mess of your flat.'

'No sir, I am referring to *Rising Damp*, the 1960s sit-com. What did you think of that?'

It's not the sort of question you expect to be asked on a quiet Sunday afternoon in the East End of London, but we manage to cobble together a consensus that it was an amiable enough comedy of its time.

Our new mate is rather more enthusiastic than that. 'I think it's the best they ever made. That Rigsby – he's always trying to get that Miss Jones, but he never will, will he?'

We agree that, Leonard Rossiter being dead and, for these purposes, irreplaceable, Rigsby never will get Miss Jones. We discuss various other vintage comedies – *Only Fools and Horses* and *One Foot in the Grave* among them – but then our interrogator drops a bombshell.

'You know what else I like? *On the Buses*. That was really good.'

That was the moment I realised I was abandoning my son among some very strange people in That London.

MY mate who is co-ordinating my escape from London has some relevant memories of Stratford Station.

'I was mugged there for 15 quid by five African lads,' he says philosophically. Thanks for the encouragement, Dave, but £15 divided by five of them? That's not even the national minimum wage they're earning there. They might even have grounds for some sort of claim against you.

It's a funny place now, Stratford. Transformed for the London Olympics, it is oddly out of scale with itself. Basically, everything is just too big. Even the steps leading up to a shopping centre the size of Bluewater look as if they were built for tens of thousands to surge along simultaneously – like extras in Eisenstein's storming of the Winter Palace – which is exactly what they were used for during the Games. When there's just you and a couple of potential muggers, it all feels a bit lonely. Despite all the assurances that everything built for the London Olympics would have a full and active life afterwards, it's a ghostly, empty quarter a few years after the end of the fun and Games. Perhaps the arrival of West Ham United as tenants of the main stadium will change that.

Way over there, back on the other side of Stratford interchange, is the number 86 stop which will put me on my way to Romford, by way of Ilford.

It looks a day's hike away. Even the rain is of Olympic proportions. It's on the news later in the day that some areas of East London and Essex have had two months' worth of rain crammed into one day. A personal wettest, if not a personal best. It is, needless to say, a bank holiday and, a few miles away, traditionally the busiest day of the Notting Hill

Carnival. You can't see a thing out of the bus windows, but the highlight of the first leg of the journey is rescuing an elderly East End geezer from a spot of bother. He gets on, not far from Stratford, obviously the worse for wear, and promptly goes to sleep. Another passenger claims to know where he should be getting off, but unfortunately he himself is getting off at the stop before. He makes arrangements with the driver to decant the old fellow and point him in the right direction. The trouble is, that even when he wakes up, he can't get out of his seat. Two of us lever him up, get him down the ramp like removal men shifting an old wardrobe and stand him on the pavement, whilst he sways gently and looks around with the air of a man who has never seen any of it before. I hope he was in approximately the right place. What if he was trying to get to the Notting Hill Carnival?

In Romford, I have a wait for the 498, not, as I had hoped, to Chelmsford, but to Brentwood, a shorter distance away. They are big in Romford on digital departure displays in bus shelters, but in the whole time I'm waiting there not a single bus turns up at its appointed and illuminated time – and this on a non-working day with traffic a good deal thinner than usual. A lesson most people learn in London and surrounding counties is to take absolutely no notice of timetables. They are there as a signal of an aspiration, not as a serious promise that they can be held to. I'm told that a London bus is regarded as on time if it arrives up to a minute early or five minutes late, which is a generous-sounding target to aim for. London Transport still missed its targets in 2014, which seems to confirm the approximate nature of its timetables.

All the same, I resort to one in Brentwood, but it is raining so hard that I misread it and turn up for the bus heading back towards London, rather than the one for

Chelmsford. That resulted in me spending a good deal longer in Brentwood than I wanted or needed. Now, this is what most people would call a typical English High Street in 2014; hardly anything that isn't part of a chain or a global conglomerate. Another indicator of the limited range of possibilities is that the best option for sitting, sheltering and sipping a coffee is a McDonald's, one of the 1,200 that have spread across the country since the first burger was flipped at Woolwich 40 years earlier.

It's halfway to Chelmsford before you really start to feel that you're properly out of London, by which time it's raining even harder. As we pull into the bus station, though, I hear the unmistakeable squelch of a flooded-out music festival. Rayleigh Folk Festival, 15 miles away, has been rained-off and abandoned, but some of the artists and a few survivors from the audience have decamped to a pub under the railway arches next to the bus station and said: 'Hey, let's do the show right here.' We don't surrender to the weather in England; we adapt to it and sing along with it.

I lose count of the number of times we cross the A12 on the last bus of the day to Colchester, but eventually there we are, with the rain still lashing down and no room booked. I try a couple of places, without success, before I do what I always do – go into a pub and ask. The Chinese barman can't think of anywhere nearby, but two lads-around-town, propping up the bar and deep into a day's serious bank holiday drinking, overhear the conversation and take over the case. Out come the mobile phones and, a couple of calls later, they've found me a place, just over the River Colne on the way out of town. I'm not sure whether I'm meant to hear one ask the other: 'Do you think we should send him there? You know, after what happened?'

'Should be alright by now,' says his mate doubtfully.

I make discreet inquiries, but never find out what horrors had taken place. There are plenty of well documented horrors in the long history of the town, however.

Colchester can claim to be the oldest town in the country, was briefly the capital of England and often the frontline between the Romans and the local tribes, most notably Boadicea's Iceni. In his book *Folk Heroes of Britain*, Charles Kightly warns that the Boadicea – or more correctly, Boudica – immortalised as the noble warrior queen in the famous statue on the Embankment, is a Victorian invention. The reality was a good deal more bloodthirsty, but then again, so were the Romans, and they took turns to massacre each other at Colchester. The Roman historian, Tacitus, wrote that: 'The Britons took no prisoners and sold no captives into slavery, and neither did they observe any of the other conventions of war. Instead they hastened to slay and to hang, to burn and to torture, almost as if they were revenging in advance the coming Roman retribution.' In other words, get your retaliation in first. Accounts of the atrocities on both sides recall nothing so much as recent events in Syria. So much for human progress.

From Roman times onwards, Colchester was a garrison town. It still is; pubs advertise special deals for students and soldiers, hopefully not on the same nights, or there could be some fresh atrocities.

My hotel is okay, apart from a slight atmosphere of something undefined having happened there. When I venture out into the continuing rain, though, I don't feel like going further than the nearest corner shop for a cheese and onion barm and a dark chocolate Kit Kat. As I'm coming back with my booty, I come across a little family group, shivering in the downpour. The man of the family is a huge fellow with a beret pulled down to his brows to try to keep the rain out of his eyes. With their Polynesian features and unpreparedness for the weather, they couldn't look more out of place. Then it strikes me. Of course, Fijians.

As I should know better than most, British Army rugby teams – league and union – are largely composed of recruits from Fiji. This must be one of those nights when, like the Roman foot-soldiers almost 2000 years ago, they wonder what the hell they're doing in Colchester.

Something stinks in Saxmundham

I RESUME the pas-de-deux with the A12 on the bus to Ipswich.

It's sufficiently confusing that, at one stage, I become convinced that we're going the wrong way on it. I eventually reassure myself that it's because I can't distinguish between Lowestoft and Felixstowe.

In fact, if I had them on my mental map of England at all, I had them the wrong way around. It didn't really matter when I had no intention of going to either place, but now it could be crucial. And then suddenly it all becomes irrelevant again, because we're going nowhere. The bus, operated by Carters Coaches, looked a particularly beat-up specimen, with cracked windows and a grunting, labouring engine, when it rolled up. Finally, on the edge of the village of Stratford St Mary, it gave up the ghost.

'Public transport,' says the driver. 'What can you expect?'

'It could be worse,' says a relentlessly upbeat woman, who seems positively grateful for the delay. 'We could be on a main road.'

We certainly aren't on a main road, but we are,

fortunately, no great distance from the company's depot at Capel St Mary, from where they send out a shiny new replacement.

'We'll only be an hour late in Ipswich,' says Mrs Grateful.

That hour is enough to condemn me to a round-the-houses travel experience to get me to Southwold. It involves going through Wickham Market and then having an hour and a half to kill in Saxmundham. I somehow doubt that I'll be going back there in a hurry.

It's a well-heeled place, a small market town, very well maintained. True, there's a charity shop on the market square, but the charity is Homes for Horses. If it had the equivalent of a pound shop, everything would be priced in guineas. In short, it fancies itself rotten. There's nothing as vulgar as a pub open in the early afternoon, so I go into a café, where they make it pretty plain that they don't fancy serving me.

'Tell him that it'll be half an hour,' I hear the boss say in a stage whisper.

Further up the street, they're a little more friendly, but reckon that they've got no bathroom I can use – which must surely be a breach of some by-law. What they can offer me is a public toilet just around the corner. 'But it might be locked up,' they say.

Sure enough, there's a big padlock on each entrance, but – how can I phrase this tastefully? – that has not dissuaded a steady stream of visitors from using it for both the purposes for which it was originally intended. So it sits there, reeking in the sunshine, not 30 yards from the chintzy little café where I've just been sitting out. I thought my corned beef and piccalilli sandwich was a bit on the pungent side. It's symbolic of something or other, that's for sure.

Route 63

It does make me reflect on a truth once pointed out to me by a plain-speaking Yorkshireman of my acquaintance: 'If tha looks like a tramp, tha'll get tret like a tramp.'

By Saxmundham standards, I look like a tramp. I've been away from home for a couple of weeks. The clothes I'm wearing have been saturated a couple of times. My shoes almost disintegrated in Colchester and I'm still going sockless. I'm struggling with a back-pack which has lost one shoulder-strap. More so than at any other time on the journey, I've got the shakes pretty bad. I've not had a drink, but I probably seem drunk. I'm not sure I would serve me; I'm just making Saxmundham look untidy. If you have partaken of a small drink, Parkinson's can make you seem as though you've partaken of a large one. That's one of the joys of the condition. You can create a bad impression much more cheaply.

While I'm on the subject, I have a complaint. I had this bloody thing before it was fashionable. There you are, trying to carve yourself a modest niche with droll observations and brittle little jokes about the condition, when out they wheel Billy Bloody Connolly and (posthumously) Robin Williams. I mean, gie's a break! Likewise in the world of sport; all I have to compete with there as a Parkinson's pin-up is Muhammad Ali. No hint of fighting out of my division there, then.

Waiting for my bus to Halesworth, I'm joined by an elderly gentleman, who is a little concerned about the time of his bus to Wickham Market.

'I haven't caught it for 40 years,' he says. 'I'm thinking the timetable might have changed.'

AT Halesworth, there's a complicated, three-bus swap manoeuvre at the railway station, but it gets me on the service to Southwold, which is very much where I want to be.

It's a place I've wanted to visit for ages, because it sounds like such an eccentric survivor from the great days of the English seaside holiday. Things look promising from the start, with the Maize Maze at Reydon; a puzzle based on a pun and, as they can't resist saying from time to time, really rather amazing. I wonder how many children there are from previous summers still wandering around inside.

At Blythburgh, there is the even more stunning sight – and, when the wind blows in the right direction, smell – of a huge free-range pig farm. I'd guess its area at about 20 football pitches, all divided into little paddocks with shelters for a sow and her litter, like a porcine suburban housing estate with all the dads out at work. At any given time there are around 2,000 sows and 20,000 pigs in total. I have to check that I haven't slipped any extra noughts in there, because it seems an awful lot of pigs. That number is almost reduced when half a dozen piglets – any one of them worth an audition for *Babe* – come rolling and tumbling delightedly out of the farm, onto the road and nearly under the bus wheels. Not all early exits are at the time of the pigs' choosing; the local paper carries a story about six pigs being shot by cross-bows in an attempt to poach their much sought-after meat.

The bus is due to drop us off at the King's Head in Southwold. The only slight disappointment is that the local brewers, Adnams, have closed the pub down, after a series of problems with it. It's part of a malaise that the outside world might not notice yet, but which seems to be obvious enough to Southwolders, if that's what they call themselves.

For the first time on my travels, my instructions tell me to aim for the lighthouse and carry on in the same direction. That might not be a great idea in most seaside towns, but Southwold's photogenic red and white lighthouse is very firmly on dry land, in the yard of Adnams' brewery tap, the Sole Bay pub. Three of its predecessors fell into the sea, because of erosion. I'm just around the corner, on the seafront, and promised a view of beach and pier, which indeed I have. I also look out across the roofs of Southwold's trademark individually painted beach huts. A few other resorts have them, but not in the same numbers and not at the same extortionate prices. It costs £20 to hire one for the day, rising to £25 in high season. As for buying one for your sole use, prepare yourself to pay a price that would buy you a terraced house in some parts of the country.

The pier might not be the longest in the realm, but it could well be the most elegant. Thanks to Carters Coaches, I'm too late to properly explore its quirky amusement arcade, with machines designed in Heath Robinson style by Tim Hunkin. Just a walk along it, though, gives you the perfect view of a miniature English resort, albeit with the sinister white dome of the Sizewell B nuclear power station peeping out incongruously from behind the far headland. In the same direction is a settlement that emphasises the provisional nature of this coast. Dunwich was once a major port; now most of it has disappeared in a series of coastal collapses and only a village-sized vestige remains.

Where Southwold pier meets the promenade there is a wall devoted to George Orwell, who spent holidays and some longer periods of his life here. Christened Eric Blair, he took the name of the river that flows through Ipswich for his pen-name. Discreetly in the bottom corner of the mural, full of quotes from *1984*, *Animal Farm* and the rest, there's a little inscription warning you that the site is protected by close circuit television. What can you possibly say about that? Except that it makes the entire journey worthwhile. It's either a blisteringly funny piece of satire or, even better, a sublime unconscious irony. On Southwold Pier, however, there is no mention of *Road to Wigan Pier* let alone 'Down and Out in Saxmundham.'

Actually, I've smartened myself up a bit. Southwold seems to politely demand it. After checking out the Sole Bay, I eat at the nearby Lord Nelson. It's the best meal of the entire trip; a whole baked plaice, topped with a dozen giant shell-on prawns, chorizo, samphire and potatoes – all for nine quid.

Seafood you expect on the east coast. Chorizo I have come to expect, because, a few years after it would have been seen as an impossibly exotic ingredient, it is now everywhere; from chorizo soup to chorizo ice cream. Fortunately, I like chorizo. I don't know how we managed without it.

On my way back from my night out, I happen upon a sight that seems to me to sum up Southwold. A pair of cottages, obviously holiday lets, both have, on their outside window sill, a neat line of children's trainers, arranged in order of size, drying out after their day on the beach. If that isn't a symbol of the lost innocence of the English seaside, here in its last resort, I don't know what is. I don't think you could get away with that in Blackpool. In fact, if there had been a nice pair of size 11s, I would have been tempted myself, given the state of my footwear. Perhaps, though, it's the suspicion that Big Brother could well be watching that keeps everybody honest.

The breakfast is also the best of the whole journey,

although I haven't the heart to ask whether any Blythburgh pigs died in order to provide it. All pigs are equal, but, come breakfast time, some are more equal than others.

My landlady is adamant about one thing, however; Southwold, as she knows it, is dying and she can't wait to get out. The character, she says, is draining out if it, because property speculators have bought up so much of it and rent it out at prices that only national chains and multi-nationals can pay. There is an inexorable force that will eventually make it like everywhere else. I'm glad I saw it while that process still had some way to go.

FOR a place that was so difficult to reach from the south, Southwold is surprisingly easy to leave to the north.

There's a bus every hour to Great Yarmouth, calling first at the village of Wangford. If that name rings a bell with you, it could be because you have a weakness for spoof country and western. The artist known as Hank Wangford was born there as plain Samuel Hutt, but adopted his home village as his stage name, performing a repertoire with his band, the Lost Cowboys, that the *New York Times* described as occupying the space 'between ridicule and reverence.' A good space to occupy.

To give you some idea of his output, his latest double CD, consisting entirely of sad songs in waltz time, includes tracks like 'I Love You So Much It Hurts Me' and 'Waltzing With Sin.' At nearby Wrentham, there is a shop called Boggis Electrical; sadly, it is closed down, an event which surely deserves to be commemorated by a Wangford composition.

'The Night the Lights Went Out at Boggis Electric' – something like that.

All this adoption of new names, whether you finish up as an Orwell or a Wangford, who in real life is a gynecologist, incidentally, is vaguely in tune with local custom and practice. Southwold's herring fishermen, for instance, invariably operated under nicknames, so that a book of portraits of these salty dogs in my hotel pictures 'Hush' Crickmore and 'Champagne' Rogers, to name but two.

It occurs to me as we head for Great Yarmouth how little I understand about East Anglia. I know the basics, like where it is and that it's not far off being as big as Wales, but I've only been there a handful of times and I've no real appreciation of what it's for, of what makes it tick. Those who love it, from Constable onwards, make great play of its big skies. To me, they merely delineate what is missing; the skies are big because there is so little breaking the horizon. It's just too damn flat and featureless. I know that some people have to live there, otherwise the island would be hopelessly unbalanced, but how is it possible to enthuse about it?

I need some local input, some interpreters who can put it in context for me, so I have a day organised in which I will actually interview people in a pre-arranged way, as opposed to just chatting and earwigging in my normal manner. In Great Yarmouth, I'm due to meet up with Keith Roberts, originally from Wigan but a long-time resident of the Yarmouth area, now living at Caister, a couple of miles down the coast. He arrived in these parts with a strange affinity for the twin-piered town of Yarmouth, however, because in a manner of speaking he's a pier himself. Keith is a singer and, way back in the 70s, he made an acclaimed LP entitled *Pier of the Realm*, so called because he was from

Wigan, which, of course, has a pier – or a bit of a protrusion into the Leeds-Liverpool Canal. Well, it seemed like a good idea at the time.

Since I hadn't seen him for at least 30 years, it also seemed like a good idea to exchange descriptions. That meant we were both looking for a big, bearded bloke with a backpack and a northern accent – and you would be surprised how many of them there are in Great Yarmouth's Wetherspoons at lunchtime on a Tuesday. Eventually, by a process of elimination, we find each other. I've already formed a few impressions of the place, some of them whilst our bus inched through slow-moving vehicles by the docks that almost amounted to a traffic jam.

'Yarmouth has an identity crisis,' says Keith. 'It can't decide whether it's a holiday resort, or a working town, or what it is.'

His view is that it isn't making much of a fist of either, although he does feel a bit of pride by association in the 'other' Nelson's Column, which stands in the romantic location of an industrial estate on the edge of town. It was originally intended to celebrate the victory at the Battle of the Nile, but the money was slow coming in and by the time it was built Nelson had died at Trafalgar. It became a memorial to him, although oddly the figure of Britannia on top looks inland rather than out to sea.

'And those stone carvings on top,' says Keith. 'Fibreglass.'

That seems to him to be symptomatic of the whole town, with all the good old stuff compromised by modern rubbish. Mind you, he's a folk singer from Wigan, so what would you expect? Keith still performs occasionally, mainly at old people's homes, of which there are plenty. There are two things he misses. One is rugby league, although he does take in the odd game at Hemel Stags when visiting relatives, and the other I could have predicted.

'I miss the hills,' he says. 'There's no hills around here. It's all so flat. They say you get the big skies, but I'm not so sure about that.'

We could have made some sort of attempt to measure the cloudless one above Yarmouth this Tuesday, but it looks perfectly standard-sized to me. Dickens set much of *David Copperfield* in Yarmouth and lived there whilst writing it. I'm sure that, if I go through arguably his most famous novel with a fine tooth comb, there will be plenty of references to big skies and excessive flatness. If Charles Dickens can do that, so can Keith Roberts. He would not be convicted by a jury of his piers.

Yarmouth is served by one of England's most ambitious bus routes, the X1, which runs all the way from Peterborough to Lowestoft (or is it Felixstowe? No, definitely Lowestoft). I struggle to think of any connection between Peterborough and Lowestoft, other than this. Indeed, I wonder how many passengers, if any, travel the full route. I'm certainly not; just as far as Norwich for me. That's far enough to show me a few glimpses of Norfolk's most celebrated landscape.

The Broads are an intricate pattern of waterways and little lakes. Not just flat round here, but flooded too. That's what happens when you extract peat too enthusiastically, as they apparently did during the Middle Ages. Dig the holes and the North Sea will come and fill them, without having to be asked twice.

In Norwich, I switch to another long-distance route – is there any other sort of route in Norfolk? – to King's Lynn. On the way, we go through Dereham, home to my recently widowed cousin, but I've found out in advance that she's away on holiday. My only other link with the area is a week-long walk on the Norfolk Coastal Path with my son and nephew some ten years or so earlier. From Hunstanton to Cromer, it rarely stopped raining and the size of the sky became difficult to gauge, because it was often so thoroughly merged with land and sea. If we woke in our various B&Bs and it hadn't quite set in for the day yet, the lads would ask me what the sky looked like.

'Enormous,' I was able to tell them. 'Abso-bloomin'-lutely enormous.'

In Lynn, as we regular visitors call it, I'm being met by someone who can explain how this punctured county holds together – and the role of the humble bus in that. Ben Colson was one of a team that took over the three buses run by a company called Norfolk Green and turned them into a fleet of 80, before flogging off the whole thriving business to Stagecoach 17 years later. He has been recommended to me as something of a bus guru. Despite selling up, partly because of health problems, he still takes a bus out occasionally for old times' sake and one of the fleet bears his name. He has bus routes in his bloodstream.

Over dinner in the village of Castle Rising, Ben outlines his busman's philosophy; that, if you hope to persuade more people on board, you have to give them more – comfier seats, friendlier drivers and the rest. He is a staunch supporter of the free bus pass, but only provided that the government stumps up the money in return. It should do, he argues, if only out of enlightened self-interest.

'For every £1 that goes into financing bus passes, £2.50 goes into the local economy,' he says.

I don't know how you'd go about substantiating that claim, but it sounds convincing. Get the old girl into town on market day for nothing and the chances are that she'll buy something while she's there. There can, however, be some severe complications.

A route Colson created along the North Norfolk Coast, known as the Hopper, proved so popular with both residents and visitors that it led to ethnic violence.

'Local people and holidaymakers were fighting over seats on the buses,' he says. 'We had to get the police out one time.'

Norfolk Green's answer to that one was ingenious. It now operates a two-tier system. People with passes issued in Norfolk are allowed to use them from 8.30; the rest of us have to wait until 9.30, by which time the locals are well on their way to wherever they're going. It seems to work quite well.

Ben has an extraordinary life in an extraordinary place. He lives in one of the villages on the Royal estate at Sandringham and it is not unknown for him to have to give way to a four-wheel drive driven by an elderly lady in a head scarf whose face you vaguely recognise from banknotes. His house used to be the first-class waiting room for the now defunct Sandringham Station. They don't have pubs in the villages on the estate; they have social clubs, where, like the Houses of Parliament, her obedient servants drink, duty-free.

He is also one of those people who, though technically retired, always seems to have six jobs to do at any one time. He is still a man the government goes to on bus-related matters, although they don't always take his advice. His other time-consuming activity is promoting the town of King's Lynn to anyone who will listen. Thus it is that I experience the *King's Lynn After Dark Tour*, learn that it was the busiest port in England in the 14th century, was the first British member of the Hanseatic League and has more listed buildings than York. What I find myself most impressed with is the Tuesday Market Place, a square that would not look out of place in any north European trading city and which has held 17,000 for concerts.

Perhaps because his old busman's instincts make him see them all as potential customers, Ben is something of an authority on the who's where of the shifting patterns of immigration into East Anglia. Apparently most of the European in-comers you see around Lynn are Lithuanian. Other Baltic and East European states have their favourite areas, whilst the Portuguese tend to cluster around Thetford. Wisbech is associated with Uzbeks, but that might have something to do with the catchy sound of Wisbechistan.

'Sometimes you can be the only native English speaker on the bus,' Ben says. That isn't quite my experience, but on the bus to Spalding the next morning there are two kids – maybe 10 and 12, brother and sister, at a guess – speaking a language I don't understand a word of. They are playing what might be an old Lithuanian clapping game, the object of which seems to be slapping the other on the head. If any Lithuanian reader recognises this description, I'd love a copy of the rules.

THE miles to the west of King's Lynn are some of the most confusing in the country.

In close proximity there are half a dozen villages with Walpole in their names and quite a few Terringtons. Then it's a series of Suttons and you're in Lincolnshire.

If the county has an image, it can perhaps be summed up in the phrase: 'Lincolnshire: Not Quite as Flat as Norfolk' which, as a Unique Selling Point, ranks right up there alongside: 'Widnes. Not as Smelly as it Used to be.'

Lincolnshire: Not As Flat As You Thought

At Spalding, you're at the heart of the Lincolnshire Bulbfields, although you wouldn't know it. The flower business is wilting badly, in the face of competition from cheaper, air-freighted blooms from Europe. Time was when coach trips used to come from all over Britain to see the tulips. There was an annual Tulip Parade that attracted over 100,000; now it's down below 40,000 and the local council has said that it is not going to fund it any more. In a few years, we'll be echoing Marlene Dietrich and Pete Seeger by asking 'Where Have All The Flowers Gone?' You don't see wooden Spalding tennis racquets any more either. Spalding boasts one transport option that I think must be unique in this country – a water taxi on the River Yelland.

Our Norfolk Green bus has been driven, very carefully, from King's Lynn by a trainee driver, who is being watched and rated by an on-board assessor. He's taken on board all the customer care mantra. You can't fault him on that; he seems personally concerned about every single one of us. Unfortunately, he's also exceptionally slow, with the inevitable consequence of missed connections in Spalding – with no tulips to look at.

The next link in the chain for me is Boston, whose parish church, known as The Stump, is visible from miles away. St Botolph's, as it is known more formally, is the biggest parish church in the country. It was Bostonians who sailed on the Mayflower and became known as the Pilgrim Fathers, so the whole town should be a monument to the mobility of peoples. The irony now is that Boston has 25 percent of its residents born in another country, the highest proportion in Britain. Bring me your poor, your huddled masses, indeed. Many of the recent arrivals have been from Poland, although it is the Portuguese who have been in the headlines, especially when they play England at football and emotions have a habit of running high. Small wonder that the town and its agricultural hinterland have proved fertile ground for the United Kingdom Independence Party. If they can't peddle their bogus analysis of England's situation here, they can't do it anywhere.

Boston's bus station is a depressing place, almost as if making it too comfortable would attract further waves from Portugal and Poland. I'm the only one on the bus for most of the journey to Lincoln, which proceeds not on the nice, straight road via Sleaford, but along a series of narrow country lanes towards Coningsby. When we get there, we find hundreds of people crowding around the perimeter fence, all scanning the skies for something or other. A little further on, there's the disorientating sight of the village of Tattershall bedecked from head to toe in the Canadian maple leaf flag. It looks exactly as though there has been a successful invasion and the locals have thrown in their lot with the invaders and are trying to ingratiate themselves with them. It comes as a bit of a shock. After all, we've fought two World Wars against the Germans and their allies and been involved in hostilities since then with enemies as diverse as North Korea, Argentina, Iceland and Iraq – just to name one World Cup group – not to mention 30-odd years of the Cold War. And it turns out that the ones we should have been watching for all the time were the sneaky Canadians, whose takeover has begun in rural Lincolnshire, possibly because of its resemblance to the Prairies.

Time for an explanatory chat with the driver, who tells me that RAF Coningsby – which is what lay beyond that tall wire-mesh fence – is hosting the visit of the only two Lancaster Bombers still in flying condition, one of which is the property of the Canadian Warplane Heritage Museum. It had crossed the Atlantic from Hamilton, Ontario, with stops at Goose Bay in Labrador, Narsarsuaq in Greenland and Keflavik, Iceland. It was going to fly alongside the RAF's one survivor and that, for aircraft enthusiasts, was pretty big news. Hence the colourful welcome awaiting them in Tattershall. The Lancaster is most celebrated for its role in the 'Dambuster' raids on Germany in 1942, which did so much to disrupt their industry.

Back on the ground and a few miles closer to Lincoln, there's an example of why you should always keep your eyes peeled on a bus journey. Had I blinked at the wrong time, I would have missed Peter Scott's shoe shop in Woodhall Spa. The whole frontage – not that there is much of it – is devoted to the claim: The Smallest Shoe Shop in Britain. Admit it; I bet you thought that the holder of that particular distinction would be somewhere, well, bigger. But no, it's in this little Victorian inland resort, in the booking office of its defunct railway station and, apart from being small, it's an awkward wedge shape. In its day, it has been a bookshop, an electrical suppliers, a jewellers and a bank. I can just imagine the conversation between the shoe sellers and the estate agents.

'It's very small.'

'Yes, but bear in mind that it will probably stretch when you've worked in it for a while.'

I toy with the idea of leaping off and replacing my leaking footwear, but there are already two people in there and it's full. There are occasional misunderstandings with people who think it is a shop selling exceptionally small shoes, presumably to elderly Chinese ladies. Not correct; normal-sized shoes, small premises.

Glad we sorted that one out.

A fairly well kept secret

LIKE the Boston Stump, Lincoln Cathedral is visible from miles away. So it should be; it was once, as far as we know, the highest building in the world, superseding the Great Pyramids at Giza. Not only that, but it is built right on top of a hill.

I know what you're thinking: A hill in Lincolnshire? Big deal. Try running up Steep Hill, as it is uncompromisingly called, with a couple of bags of shopping, and tell me that. So how does somewhere which was once important and prestigious enough to boast a world-class building, looking down loftily on the rest of the globe's squat little man-made structures, become such a backwater?

Decline set in during the 14th century and the cathedral lost its tallest spire in 1549, when it rotted and collapsed and was never replaced. There were also geographical oddities, like the city being split into Up Hill and Down Hill, the latter prone to flooding and plague. The whole city is in the wrong place; too far from the sea – and that at Skegness, labelled as England's most impoverished coastal town in a recent survey – and away from main transport routes.

What those failings have produced, however, is a remarkably well-preserved area at the top of the hill, as handsome as it is historic. It has a delightful atmosphere and is not usually completely over-run by tourists, like York, for instance. My youngest daughter lives roughly where Up Hill meets Down Hill, not far from the river basin, Brayford Pool. No tourists down her street, but no plague either. She took her degree in illustration at Lincoln University and liked the place so much that she has never left. I can't say I blame her. She has gradually built herself a role as trainee barrista and unofficial illustrator-in-residence at Lincoln's leading café; Up Hill, needless to say. I'd like to think that, if one of her customers on a pavement table was attacked by a seagull (see Brighton chapter) she would dash outside and fight it off with a brush. She has a wide and interesting circle of friends. The city is good to look at. It has a thriving arty-crafty and music scene and plenty of chorizo. Let me elaborate.

It has been a joke between the two of us since she went there that we really must go to a Spanish restaurant not far from where she now lives. For one thing, it advertises a new hybrid – Lincolnshire tapas. It cries out to be tried, but for years now we have been thwarted. We've turned up on nights when it was closed; on nights when it was supposed to be open, but was closed. We've rolled up twice to find that they've gone on impulsive, last-minute holidays. We've gone there when we've been personally assured that it would be open, only to find it closed for a single night, due to unforeseen circumstances.

Sophie meets me at the bus station – Down Hill – with the good news that she has checked and double-checked and it's definitely open that night. We get there and, of course, it's closed; due to unforeseen holidays or something of the sort.

The difference between Lincoln and other cities is that just down the street from the endless mañana of our elusive restaurant is an expanse of green fields called West Common. Go uphill from there and you get to the Castle and Cathedral in the area known historically as The Bail. It has recently been rebranded as The Cathedral Quarter. Towns and cities are keen on quarters these days; some of them have as many as five, which is quite an achievement when you think about it. If you are lucky enough to have a public library, you have the makings of a Literary Quarter. A library and a theatre gives you a Cultural Quarter. Down the hill at Brayford Pool, you have the Water Quarter, but Sophie and I have dined out up the hill so often that I think of it as the Daughter Quarter. In recognition of its particularly gory past, Colchester really ought to have a Slaughter Quarter.

Back in the Tapas Quarter, the interesting new place we fancy is full, but yes, we can have a table outside if we want. And there we sit, with a stunning view of Cathedral, Castle and clear blue sky, eating chorizo simmered in red wine, accompanied by some of the best buskers you'll ever hear. To start with, there's just a guy playing pretty tasty guitar, until another strolls along, whips out a harmonica and joins in. Then, from the opposite direction, a fellow ambles along and sings the blues for a while. It might have been choreographed, but Lincoln's the sort of place where it could happen quite naturally.

Lincoln gets its share of visitors, especially for its Christmas Market; street stalls promoting local breweries and a Big Wheel – what's not to like? But, compared to the big tourist attractions, it is left to mind its own business. As for its slight sense of unreality, one reason was suggested a few weeks after I passed through. Out of all the possible candidates, the first council in the country to decide that it had such a problem with so-called 'legal highs' that they needed to be banned was Lincoln. That might account for the slightly glazed expression you see there rather more frequently than in most places. Legal highs? Not in the centre of Lincoln they're not.

I've had a masterplan for some time to see my offspring based strategically around the globe so that I can go and visit them. I've got one in London; I could do with one in Sydney, preferably in Manly or the Eastern Suburbs.

I've got one in Saudi Arabia, which isn't really much use to me, but I'm as pleased as punch to have one in Lincoln. And next time, we might try the brand new Lithuanian restaurant we noticed on the way to the bus station; Down Hill but rather smart-looking. I bet they'll be open.

The town that dares not spell its name

THE bus the following morning does not head north on the arrow-straight A15 – the Romans' Ermine Street. Instead, it weaves around in a way that has become familiar to me on this trip, picking up the odd person in one village, dropping one off in the other. That denied me a look at a place that could have been the most memorable of the whole expedition. Around 11 miles north of Lincoln on the A15 is the village of Spital On The Street. That's an on-the-spot £50 fine where I come from.

As a problematic name, however, that is as nothing compared with the town another dozen miles towards the Humber. As far as I know, Scunthorpe is the only town in Britain to fall foul of internet service providers' obscenity filters. At various times, it has been rendered as S****thorpe or Scoonthorpe. To my mind, either of those alternatives is considerably more offensive, but the computer doesn't know how to make these judgements. Its natives and neighbours call it Scunny and I'm not sure whether that's better or worse. The issue of over-zealous filters is apparently known in the computer world as the Scunthorpe problem, which just goes to show that everywhere is famous for something.

Actually, Scunthorpe claims to be a place of a type I've never heard of before – the industrial garden town. If that sounds full of potential contradictions, then it probably is, but, in effect, it is an old iron and steel town with a lot of parks. After what seems rather too long in the town's bus station, I pick up the service to Hull and find myself ear-wigging on a conversation between two young blokes about a mutual friend who has just become a father.

'I asked him what it's like, being a dad,' says one. 'He says it has its good points and its bad points, but he hasn't actually seen the baby yet.'

'What's the bad points then, when he 'ant even seen it?'

Seems a fair question. Both of them are going up towards the Humber, in search of cash-in-hand work. They are agreed on one thing; there's nothing going in Scunny. The gardens are nice, though, and it seems an exceptionally lucky town. The first couple to win a million pounds on the National Lottery TWICE come from Scunthorpe; nobody sniggers at their address.

Until 1981, getting to Hull from here involved either a lengthy detour inland via Goole or the ferry from Barton-upon-Humber. There was also a hovercraft, but it only lasted a few months and was plagued by technical faults. Then they built the Humber Bridge and nothing was ever quite the same again.

It was one of those structures that actually changes the geography of a region, turning distant neighbours into close ones. I suppose the Forth Road Bridge must have done the same for the Kingdom of Fife. On our itinerary, however, it threw together two areas that appear to want absolutely nothing to do with each other – North Lincolnshire and East Yorkshire. They even combined the two between 1974 and 1996 as the county of Humberside, but nobody really believed in its existence. You still can't even refer to

Humberside as a geographic entity without attracting angry letters from East Yorkshire Nationalists, written in green ink with lots of CAPITALS and exclamation marks!!!!! On top of that, the River Humber itself doesn't get the recognition it deserves, because before it gets into its stride it splits into two and becomes the Trent and the Ouse. Everyone knows the Trent, but, strictly speaking, it's only a tributary of the Humber. Look at the map in a slightly different way and we would have Stoke on Humber and Burton on Humber. And Humberside would continue deep into rural Staffordshire. Alternatively, you could call it the Trent all the way to the sea and we would have Hull and Hull Kingston Rovers playing each other in the Trentside derby. Better leave things as they are, perhaps. It would only be muddying the waters and they, in all conscience, are already muddy enough.

Whatever you call it, the Humber is an impressively broad river as it approaches Hull; in fact, there are those who insist that it is not a river at all, but an estuary. Be that as it may, it's a mile wide between Barton-upon-Humber and Hessle, the route of an old ferry and of the Humber Bridge. It's a graceful as well as a mighty structure and going across it on a double decker is more an experience than it is a bus ride.

It compares well with one alternative way of doing it. Swimmers who have dodged the toll are legion, but in 2005 a 6ft 9in Hull man named Graham Boanas became the first person in modern times to wade across the submerged mud at low tide. The bridge was the longest single span in the world when it opened; it is now only seventh, which shows what a bridge-building boom there has been, some of them no doubt bringing equally reluctant neighbours closer together. Naturally, the Humber Bridge remains the area's most popular suicide spot.

Route 63

Landfall is at Hessle, a place I wasn't expecting to visit again for some time, after my bus left it behind by turning right for the city of Kingston Upon Hull.

A Hull of a Night

HULL has such a bad name that they only use a third of it, the Kingston and the Upon being kept locked away for use on special occasions only.

To those who don't know the place, it is a by-word for industrial decline – that industry being fishing – and provincial isolation. True enough, it has its rough council estates, its rougher boozers and a drinking and fighting culture that seems to hark back to the heydays of the trawlers. Its strange accent is one of the easiest in Britain to mimic and its poet laureate is gloomy old, screwed-up Philip Larkin, whose most cheerful line is: 'Man hands on misery to man.'

On the other hand, it is a genuinely maritime city, with strong and visible influences from the continent. It even has a street – The Land of Green Ginger – that is straight out of the pages of the Brothers Grimm. I have a theory that it isn't a part of Yorkshire at all, or even of Northern England, but an off-shore branch office of continental Europe. It's like going abroad, but also, to me, a little like coming home. I've timed my arrival to coincide with the Humberside rugby league derby between Hull and Hull KR and, as the bus goes past the KC Stadium – as in Kingston Communications, the people who brought you another Hull oddity, the cream phone box – I couldn't be happier. I might be a hundred miles from where I live, but I feel like I've suddenly tapped into a shared energy supply.

First things first, starting with finding a bed. There are a number of possibilities clustered around the shiny new bus station, attached to one of England's more romantically-named train termini, Hull Paragon. I find a plain but adequate room at a bargain £25 and congratulate myself on my frugality.

In the pub across the street, I hear a guttural language I vaguely recognise but can't quite place. Lithuanian? Basque? Albanian? East Hull? None of the above. Then the answer floats across from nights in the bars of Ostend and Bruges; it's Flemish. Not, as it might sound, the mother tongue of Spital on the Street, but of half of Belgium. The explanation, as so often in Hull, is a sporting one. The previous night, Hull City had played the Belgian side, KSC Lokeren, in the Europa Cup. The Flemings, not to be confused with the French-speaking Walloons, were stragglers from that match, who had been persuaded by the Rovers fans who had adopted them to give this strange local game a try.

It might be both strange and local, but, even the day after Hull City had been knocked out of Europe for the first time, rugby league commanded five pages of the *Hull Daily Mail*. No wonder I feel at home here; always have, always will, and never more so than at the Humberside derby. There are people who will tell you, at great and tedious length, that this is the only true derby in rugby league, because it pits together two clubs from the same city. That doesn't quite make it unique, although Leeds versus Hunslet hardly counts as a regular rivalry any more.

I suppose I saw my first Hull derbies in the late '70s and early '80s, when they were the two best and best supported teams in the country, and I've been hooked on the fixture since Rovers joined Hull in Super League. Even though there's absolutely nothing riding on it this time, with both clubs experiencing deeply mediocre seasons, the sense of anticipation is palpable. For once, there are no Sky cameras; it's a thoroughly parochial occasion.

One of the myths about the Hull rivalry is that the supporters of the two clubs hate each other. They both play along with it cheerfully enough. When there was wild talk of a merger, Hull fans sang: 'We're black, we're white. We'll never merge with shite.' But that's just jovial banter. There are too many families with a supporter of each club, too many people from East Hull who now live in the West and vice versa. Even the two clubs started life on opposite sides of the River Hull. So there is no real geographical divide and certainly no poisonous religious element, like Rangers and Celtic. It means that the two sets of fans can enjoy cordially insulting each other over a few pints before and after the game. Try doing that with Liverpool and Manchester United.

I expect the city will resist any attempt to rebrand it as a unified, harmonious community. I noticed the other day that the old curmudgeon, Larkin, with his casual racism and misogyny, had been exposed in a new study as rather a jolly versifier and they didn't like that piece of revisionism in Hull one little bit. What next? Andrew Marvell the Atheist or Wilberforce and his Slaves? A bowdlerised re-write of Larkin's most notorious lines, perhaps? 'They do their best, your mum and dad.'?

I travel to the match on a bus with an extended family group that is largely red and white but with a sprinkling of black and white to keep things interesting. They can be equally rude about each other's team, because they've both had a crap season, so everyone's happy. There are 18,000 others at the KC and we see the worst Humberside derby of recent years. The one thing you can guarantee from the fixture is a full measure of commitment and intensity, but that is missing this time because Rovers simply don't turn up and go down meekly to a 28-0 defeat. They finish ninth, with Hull FC a point behind in 11th. Mediocre at best, with even the old mantra about local bragging rights ringing hollow. Neither of them has anything to brag about.

What was at stake is better described as local apologising rights. The season was so disappointing on both banks of the River Hull, that it felt like time to think the unthinkable, say the unsayable: Can the city support two Super League teams? We have tended to assume over the last few years that, with its plethora of amateur clubs, its tribal support, its five pages in the local paper, that it can. But how many really top-flight players does it produce? Not enough, on the evidence of this match. No doubt I'll see a proper Hull derby next season and I'll be a true believer again, but these were the mutinous thoughts I was entertaining as I boarded the shuttle bus after the game. The amount of red and white on the bus was evidence of where it was going; into the city centre, obviously, for them to pick up connections for East Hull. After about 20 minutes, though, it is apparent that something is badly wrong. When I peer out of the window on the top deck, I can't see anything I recognise at all.

'Where's this bus going?' I ask the red and white couple directly in front.

'Hessle Park and Ride,' they tell me. 'Non-stop.'

'But that's West Hull,' I argue, hoping that it might be them that's lost, not me. But no, they might support Rovers but they live in Brough, which is as far West as you can get without dropping off the edge of the known world and into Yorkshire. Another example of how the Great Divide on Humberside does not follow geographical lines.

That's all very well, but it doesn't get me back to my luxury £25-a-night city centre hotel. Nor are there any city centre buses from Hessle at that time of night. Derek and Jane from Brough, the couple sitting in front of me, see my quandary and insist on taking me there – a very rugby league thing to do. It gives them a chance to unburden themselves to a stranger on the subject of Rovers' limp display, but basically they're doing it because they're good guys. They run a gardening business and, if ever you need your privets trimming, I warmly recommend Cutting Hedge Garden Solutions of Brough. Not only is it run by good people, but they also know the value of a good pun.

What I know the value of by this stage is a good night's sleep. It is with that in mind that I repair to my third floor room. It's been a long day and I'm ready for an epic kip. I'm as snuggly as Lenny Henry in a Premier Inn, with just the gentle sounds of the night – haunted cries from the fish-docks, distant police sirens, the occasional Robins fan sobbing in the gutter – to lull me off. Just to settle myself, I read some early reaction on the *Hull Daily Mail*'s website, where one Hull FC supporter is offering the following advice: 'Don't open your gob, until you've done the job, you dobbins.'

All is well in Kingston-upon-Hull.

Then, in the early hours of the morning, all hell breaks loose. It starts with one very angry man, running up and down the corridor outside my room, bellowing for someone or other to come out. Then he starts banging on doors, including mine, and it doesn't sound like his bare hand or even his boot he's doing it with. More like (gulp) an axe.

Now, I'm pretty confident it's not me he's after, but I have a precautionary scroll through my memory to check whether I've written anything lately that was particularly disrespectful to the city, either of its rugby teams, or even its football club. No, there doesn't seem to be anything that would attract the attention of a mad axeman. What to do, then? I could stick my head out into the corridor and say: 'Excuse me, could you keep the noise down? I've got to catch a bus to Whitby in the morning.' I could, but it doesn't seem advisable. Then there are police sirens a lot closer to the hotel, which is starting to seem not such a bargain deal, and a lot more people shouting in the corridor. There's only one thing to do. Stick on your iPod, turn the volume up to 11 and select something appropriate by a Hull group, like the first Watersons album, *Frost and Fire*. By the time that finishes, the worst of the hubbub has died down, apart from one voice asking again and again as he is dragged towards the lift: 'What have I done? What HAVE I done? What exactly have I DONE?'

The following morning, I ask a nervous looking man on the front desk what was going on, because it had sounded to me like a murder taking place.

'Nothing like that,' he said. 'We just had a spot of bother with a couple of guests.'

He said it in a matter-of-fact way that implied that it happened every weekend. Perhaps it does.

BEFORE there was Hull, there was Beverley. When Hull was little more than a quay on the riverbank, used for exporting wool to Europe, Beverley had already had its minster for 500 years. It still fancies itself as the senior partner, although it is now little more than a 20th of the size.

The evidence of that Saturday morning on the bus station is that Hull people love a day-trip there, and to

Bridlington, Filey and Scarborough beyond. If I had time, I would be repeating a foray I had made in the past, catching the bus to Easington and walking to Spurn Point. If you are addicted to that 'end of the earth' feeling, then Spurn, which is a slender, stony spit sticking out into the grey-brown water where the mouth of the Humber meets the North Sea, has it in trumps. Nobody seems to be going there, but there are plenty of takers for Beverley.

You can't blame them. It's another of England's exquisite small cathedral cities, if you will excuse me for glossing over the difference between a cathedral and a minster. The designation minster, as in Beverley, York and nearby Howden, denotes an origin as a monastery, although some parish churches have been promoted to minster status in recent years. They include some unlikely-sounding contenders, like Great Yarmouth and Dewsbury.

Only one of Beverley's medieval gates survives, but the place is full of quaint old buildings, atmospheric streets and some fine traditional pubs. One of them, the White Horse, more often known as Nellie's, after a previous landlady, is still lit by gas. There aren't many pubs that can claim that, even in Yorkshire. No time to linger, though, because there is a tight connection to Driffield and Scarborough.

Driffield, sometimes known as Great Driffield, to distinguish it from Little Driffield next door, is in the Yorkshire Wolds. That didn't keep me on the edge of my seat, though, because I had traversed the Lincolnshire Wolds without noticing them. I clearly need to sharpen up my wold view. Driffield is built on the typical North Yorkshire template, with a main street broadening into a market square. No livestock market these days, though; the foot and mouth epidemic closed it down in 2001 and it never re-opened.

Scarborough, 20 miles away, is the biggest holiday resort on the east coast. Scarborians believe that the town was founded by Viking raiders, although I understand that the evidence for this is scanty. What is certain is that it is the subject of one of the most durable folk-songs in the English language, 'Scarborough Fair.' Simon and Garfunkel made the most famous version of it, Paul Simon having got it from the distinguished folkie, Martin Carthy, who, by coincidence, now lives just up the coast at Robin Hood's Bay.

The day's journey could be turned into a dramatic expedition. It started yards from the glossy new home of the Hull Truck Theatre, whose writer in residence, John Godber, was responsible for *Up 'n' Under*, *Bouncers* and many, many more. I once interviewed Godber about the success of the first of those two plays. He was new in town, he told me, and he had an empty theatre to fill. It was either German expressionism or a play about rugby league. The bus pulls in a couple of streets away from the Stephen Joseph Theatre, where most of Alan Ayckbourn's astounding output of over 70 plays has been premiered and where he was artistic director until 2009.

There is a lovely story about Ayckbourn, which is none the less illuminating for being apochryphal. He was walking through the familiar streets of Scarborough one day, when he was stopped by a friendly elderly resident.

'Excuse me asking,' he said, 'but aren't you that Alan Ayckbourn?'

'Well, yes I am.'

'The one who wrote all those plays, performed all over the world? There must be a bit of brass in that.'

'Er, it's not bad, thanks.'

'Can I ask you one thing then? How come you never moved to Bridlington?'

Route 63

For real-life drama, it would be hard to beat events in Scarborough in 1993. That was the year the curtains came down on the Holbeck Hall Hotel. In fact, the curtains, the windows, the walls and eventually the whole building came down, as the town's only four-star establishment ended its precarious life by slipping into the sea. A classic case of erosion, you might think, just like those pathways shearing off into the English Channel that we encountered earlier in this journey; the council said different, blaming it on 'soil creep,' which is another thing altogether. When the owners tried to sue them for not protecting the cliff on which it stood, the case failed because the problem was found to be due to strata shifting under the building. The effect was much the same and the Holbeck Hall became a tourist attraction as people came to watch more of it slide over the edge. Now there is little but an information board to show where it used to stand.

I get some sustenance from the greasiest of greasy spoons, across the road from the bus stops, and I'm off to Whitby. The first major settlement is Robin Hood's Bay, the first glimpse of which, as we drop down from the main road, is as good as anything on the entire trip. By the way, do not on any account confuse Robin Hood's Bay with Robin Hood Airport, which is close to Doncaster, a good 70 miles away – unless you want to be hit with a very big taxi fare.

It's a measure of the portability of the Robin Hood legend that a reference to the green-clad outlaw, robbing the rich to give to the poor, can crop up just about anywhere in the country. If he was a real, historic figure, he was a singularly well-travelled one for his time. Among the places with a claim on him are York, Wakefield, Cumbria, Richmond in Surrey, Nottingham and South Yorkshire. The airport has a more solid connection than most, via the nearby Barnsdale

Forest, from which he is supposed locally to have operated. From the airport, by the way, you can fly not only to holiday resorts in Spain and Turkey, but also to five cities in Poland and to Vilnius, the capital of Lithuania, Riga and Bucharest. A little clue there to the changes in the local demographics.

Bay or Bay Town, as locals call it, has a more tenuous claim on Robin Hood. One of the more obscure ballads in his canon describes him seeing off a gang of French pirates who had come ashore to pillage the village. That was enough to make a connection that stuck. Fishing and smuggling were the traditional occupations, the latter of which has a touch of the Robin Hood ethos about it. Nowadays, RHB is best-known as the eastern finishing point of Alfred Wainwright's Coast to Coast Walk. Until the money ran out, anyone turning up at a pub in the village called the Bay Hotel, right on the edge of the North Sea, after completing the hike was entitled to a free half, paid for by the money Wainwright had left behind the bar many years before. My dad claimed his beer when he arrived there in his 70s, but he says that if you kept going back repeatedly, over several days, they smelt a rat.

It's a glorious looking place and the X93 is a much better way of getting there than tackling its over-stretched car parks. A 20-strong group of hikers, who sound to me like they come from Middlesbrough, assemble at the bus stop and pile aboard. One thought strikes me: What a wonderful place to have within a bus ride of where you live. No chance to overnight there this time, because Whitby is still calling.

As we approach, there's a distinct feeling of there being something special happening this particular Sunday. For one thing, there is something close to a traffic jam building up. For another, just about everyone seems to be in costume of one sort or another. There are three discernible groups: a lot of people dressed as pirates, parties of what must surely be hen-weekenders and gloomy groups of Goths. 'No,' they say at the information office. 'I can't see you finding anything for tonight.' Now, in my experience, the usefulness of a tourist information office is in inverse proportion to its size. The bigger it is, the more clueless they are. This one is the size of a small whaler.

They make one cursory phone call, which is apparently sufficient to confirm that the whole town is full.

'What about pubs?' I ask them. 'Surely there's some of them with rooms.

'Well, we don't really bother with pubs.'

What about all the hotels and guest houses I could see up on the cliffs? Surely they couldn't all be full as well?

'We don't bother with them either. You could walk up and have a look.'

So I walk up and have a look. Wherever I turn, there are signs reading 'Vacancies.' I select the one with the best view of the harbour – and the information office – and book in.

They were right about one thing, though. It was one heck of a busy Sunday on the narrow streets of Whitby. When I looked across the harbour to the 199 steps up to Whitby Abbey, they resembled nothing as much as a broken-down escalator, with nobody at all moving onward or upward. The ruined abbey is a compulsory climb for a lot of people, especially the Goths, because of its *Dracula* connections. I'd already sunk my teeth into it on a previous visit, so I didn't feel obliged to take a second bite.

Bram Stoker published his great Gothic horror novel in 1897, partly inspired by a visit to Whitby, and was responsible for the growth of a worldwide vampire industry that only gathered pace after his death in 1912. An Irish-born theatrical manager and personal assistant to the legendary

actor Sir Henry Irving, Stoker partly based the story on
Hungarian folk tales. Some of the action takes place in
Whitby and that has been enough to turn the town into a
place of pilgrimage for Goths, especially on two festival
weekends in April and November.

The original Goths – Ostrogoths and Visigoths – were
Germanic tribes who played an important role in the Fall of
the Roman Empire. In the late 1980s, the name was adopted
by a distinctive sub-culture that emerged from the Fall of the
Punk Empire. They are certainly recognisable, with their
white faces and black clothes. They seem to attract a certain
amount of hostility and persecution; the 2007 festival was
dedicated to Sophie Lancaster, a girl from Bacup who was
killed for being a Goth. They can be a sinister looking lot, but
Whitby likes them well enough. Mind you, they contribute
an estimated £1.1 million per annum to the local economy,
which helps a place to tolerate you.

They must create a curiously monochrome effect
when they are here in their numbers in November. Even in
the August sunshine, which is not really their natural setting,
there's enough of them to swell the throng. Apart from the
usual tattoos and piercings, I notice that quite a few Goths
favour jewelry made from the local black jet. This stuff first
became popular as Victorian mourning jewelry, so there's
something undeniably appropriate about it. Say what you
like about the Goths, but they've certainly got a penchant for
a pendant.

Also out in force are the pirates. You can hardly turn
a corner without running into nautical types with wooden
legs and parrots on their shoulders going 'Aaaar, Jim lad!' It's
all part of a themed weekend and it looks almost too much
fun. Whole families of Jack Sparrow lookalikes are
brandishing their cutlasses and making strangers walk the

plank. It's meant to be a celebration of Whitby's whole sea-faring heritage, but you know what pirates are like. They always take over.

Whitby's most illustrious sailor by far, however, was Capt James Cook, who learned his stuff on collier ships sailing up to the Tyne and down the east coast to London. It was a bit of a leap from that to leading the first British expedition to Australia, but he managed it. He led three voyages there, but on the third there was a bit of a misunderstanding in Hawaii and he was killed and, according to local practice, baked.

His family home in Great Ayton was dismantled and taken, stone by stone, to be rebuilt in Melbourne in the 1930s, but there is a monument to his memory on the cliffs near my guest house and I go to pay my respects. Apart from all the other consequences of his explorations, he gave names to the natural features he observed. Botany Bay is his, and so are Port Jackson and Moreton Bay. Sometimes the name chosen seems to stem from a state of mind, rather than the topography, as with Cape Flattery and Weary Bay. His name still strikes a chord with just about every visitor, although perhaps not as thunderous a one as Robert Newton's 'Aaaah, Jim lad!' in the film of *Treasure Island*, although Robert Louis Stevenson's yarn is set in Bristol.

The third sub-group adding colour – or in the Goths' case, the lack of it – to the day are what seem like a couple of dozen hen parties. Wander any distance and you find yourself, quite literally, tripping over them. What would you say was the biggest change in the ground rules of life over the last 20 years or so? The internet, the four-point try, the demolition of the Berlin Wall? None of the above, in my humble opinion; it's the way young women now get drunker and much, much louder than men.

I feel about 150 years old writing this, but it's an observable fact and, if you want to prove it to yourself, go to Whitby when the hens are out and about and spreading their wings. I've no doubt that the same applies in other attractive towns, but a combination of the sea air and the claustrophobic streets around the harbour seems to make it more potent here than in most places. Throw the Goths and the Long John Silvers into the mix, add the families taking advantage of the last weekend of the school holidays, and you've got one very crammed little town. That's especially true of the pubs. What you want is somewhere you can sit and watch the world bustle past, but the chances of finding it are slim and there's a risk of dehydration setting in. Then I notice, pointing down an alleyway towards the harbour, a little sign for the Whitby Friendly Amateur Rowing Club. Visitors welcome. Well, it would be rude not to go in, wouldn't it?

The club is not much more than a wooden shed with a bar at one end, but down a couple of rickety steps there's a terrace with as good a view of the harbour as you could wish and plenty of tables and chairs. It feels like privileged access and it is as friendly as its name suggests. I don't know how much actual rowing goes on here; it could be a convenient fiction, like the Fleet Street Golf Club, which existed, in the days of restricted opening times, largely to slake the very considerable thirsts of journalists after hours. No need for any of that subterfuge now, of course, but it still feels like a haven.

Elsewhere, it sometimes seems as though the whole of Whitby is queuing for something or other. The best queue of the lot is at the Magpie Café, an establishment so laden down with awards for the world's best fish and chips that there must be a danger of it sliding exhausted down into the water, like the Holbeck Hall Hotel. The Magpie isn't a chippy, in my book. It's a restaurant which happens to make a feature of the great British takeaway meal and which has its own carry-out counter next door. The one unifying factor is that they both have monster queues stretching out of their doors and round the block. It's an insanely popular place to eat what remains, chicken tikka masala notwithstanding, Britain's most popular takeaway. In Whitby, at any rate, its position seems secure.

Year Zero for fish and chips was 1860. That was the year when a restaurant in London began serving fried, battered fish in the style favoured by Jewish refugees from Portugal and Spain. The same year, a stall opened on Oldham's Tommyfield Market selling what we would now call chips. It is not known how and when the two got together, but they were always destined to meet and marry. Mossley, to the east of Manchester, claims the first actual chippy.

I imagine that, then as now, it could be delicious or it could be a soggy mess. The best I've ever had was on the Pittwater in Australia, but that's rather a long way to go, even further than the end of this damned queue. I don't care how good it's supposed to be, I'm not standing in line for haddock and chips. The trouble is that even chippies and fishy eateries that have won only relatively minor awards – they've all won some – are packed to the gunnels. There are enough little fishing boats bobbing in the harbour to imply that the catch is going straight from the North Sea to your plate. Eventually, I settle for a humble establishment which has only got a third-place rosette from the *Whitby Gazette* to show for its efforts. It was a bit average and rather expensive for what it was. I got talking to a couple later that evening who had found a decent place with only a half-hour waiting list. They complimented the man in charge on the freshness of his fish.

'Thank you,' he said. 'Flown in frozen from Germany.'

AN early start, taking advantage of the unrestricted bus pass hours on a Sunday. I really think it would break my heart to have to pay a bus fare at this stage.

No sooner are you out of Whitby – passing the biggest car boot sale I've ever seen en route – than you're on the North Yorks Moors. I was vaguely aware of their existence, but what surprised me was the way they came right up to the road, or, on some sections, right over the cliff and down onto the beach. It's not a juxtaposition I'm used to seeing on the other side of the country. Near Cook's birthplace of Marton, now swallowed up by the outskirts of Middlesbrough, there's the distinctive shape and evocative name of Roseberry Topping, the hill he used to climb to build up his stamina.

Middlesbrough – it's important to this itinerary. It's my defence to any misplaced accusations that I've only gone to nice places on this trip. Middlesbrough's best friends wouldn't claim that it was a beautiful place, but there is something spectacular and of epic proportions about its rise and fall.

In 1801, it consisted of one farm, with a population of 25. The discovery of iron ore nearby saw it grow more rapidly than any other industrial town. It acquired the mock-classical, unofficial title of Ironopolis. Men flocked to work in its foundries and engineering works. One third of Britain's iron was produced on Teeside. The steel for the Sydney Harbour Bridge was cast here by the local company, Dorman Long. Along with the rest of the British iron and steel industry, there is little of it left now. You would be nearer the mark to call it

Rustopolis. In 1939, though, there was enough to make Middlesbrough the first strategic target to be bombed in the Second World War. Now it is chemicals that employ the biggest slice of the population. Whenever I've been, though, its town centre has looked particularly down at heel and sorry for itself. It always ranks high in the *Crap Towns* books; mind you, they rated Hull as the crappiest of all in 2003, so what do they know?

On weekdays, Middlesbrough has what must be one of the best bus services in Britain; every half hour, express to Newcastle in a mere 80 minutes. It seems to be well used as a commuter service. The free newspaper, *The Metro*, carries a daily panel labelled 'Rush Hour Crush'. It deals mainly in budding relationships on the Tube, but smitten Geordies are muscling in. Take this example from the 29 October edition:

> To the cute girl with short dyed hair and Northumbria University pullover on the X9. You got on at Middlesbrough and you bumped into me when you got off at Gateshead. I wish you weren't in such a rush to get off the bus. Maybe if I see you again we could go for a coffee to start the morning.
>
> *Dark-haired Guy With His Mum.*

I don't give that one much of a chance of blossoming, although it makes an interesting contrast with the paragraph next to it:

> To the 5ft tall-ish fella with the cowboy hat and Bermuda shorts on the No. 37 bus to Brixton. Do you fancy (half) a pint sometime?
>
> *Your Biggest Fan.*

As so often, things are not quite so straightforward on a Sunday.

The British Sunday has changed out of all recognition over the last few decades. When I was a boy, it was, even in less than fanatically religious families like ours, a bit like being under house arrest. It was as though the object of the exercise was to make it so dull and restrictive that you were relieved to get back to work or school on Monday. Now you can watch sport, dine out, spend 12 hours in the pub, visit a massage parlour; even, should you be that way inclined, go shopping. You can even still go to church and, of course, there are plenty of people who have to go to work.

The one thing that has not kept pace with these changes is transport. Although there are all these activities calling us with their siren song, the bus timetables continue to treat the population as though it is still in a state of lock-down. Middlesbrough to Newcastle is a good example; childishly simple on a Monday, fiendishly difficult on a Sunday. No trace of any direct buses to the Toon; in fact, despite the shuttle service there during the week, they seem to have brought in specially-trained Sunday staff, who do that old bus station trick of making you unsure that your destination actually exists. In the end, I settle for a bus to Durham, on the grounds that it's roughly in the right direction and a pretty pleasant place.

Oops, there I go again. At least, it's usually pretty pleasant. I do recall covering a cricket match there one summer and it raining so hard after the close of play that the River Wear flooded, the doors of the pub I was in were quickly sand-bagged and nobody could get in or, in my case, out. There's worse ways to spend a few hours. Durham is dominated by its cathedral and its castle; which, to be fair, would dominate a bigger city. I always fancied, but never quite got to the Durham Miners' Gala. It would almost be worth going to still, if only as an outstanding example of a big event shrunken and withered by changing times.

I grab the first bus with Newcastle on it and fondly imagine that all the thinking for the day is done. Not a bit of it. As I follow our route on my map, I'm thinking 'What am I doing here?'

It's like Cook's Tour of the Durham Coalfield. We go through the village of Annfield Plain twice, which, although it doesn't look the worst place in the world, seems a little excessive. Sadly, the nearest we get to the unforgettably named Pity Me is a couple of sign-posts pointing plaintively into the distance. We must be close to the even more self-deprecatingly christened No Place. There is still the issue of the settlement on Hadrian's Wall which is called Once Brewed if you approach it from one direction and Twice Brewed if you come at it the other way. How incorrigibly Geordie is that? And how appropriate, because these are people who like to underline and emphasise every point of difference between themselves and the rest of the country. The Angel of the North puts down a marker of a different kind, standing over the A1 and declaring that you are now entering a distinctive part of Britain. For confirmation of that, you just need to get into conversation, on any subject at all, with a Geordie. They see the world through a different lens.

Take football, for instance; to the rest of the world, it is all too apparent that Newcastle United are the great under-achievers of sport and always will be. With all their advantages – a captive audience, a productive hinterland and local dominance, even the modern rarity of a city centre ground – they have hardly ever won anything. Plenty of Geordie players have bulging trophy cabinets, but not as a

160

result of playing for Newcastle. The most extreme example was Burnley's Championship-winning side of 1960, scouted and signed, almost to a man, from the North East. A few years before that, Newcastle won the FA Cup three times in the 1950s and then the Inter-Cities Fairs Cup in 1968. Since then, nothing; and yet, if you talk to any Geordie, you will be left in no doubt that the Toon are the biggest club in the world and that 50-odd years of failure are a mere blip, an aberration. You have to admire them, really, for their unshakable belief in the face of reality.

As it is with football, so it is with beer. The Geordies have made a cult of Newcastle Brown Ale and they have persuaded an astonishing number of outsiders to sign up to it. To the non-Geordie palate, it's an unpleasantly sweet, mass produced drink with iconic packaging. It isn't even as strong as it's cracked up to be; a mere 4.7 per cent – equivalent to a typical best bitter – and you get some hops with that.

When it was first launched in the 1920s, it was considerably stronger. In its weaker form, however, it became unaccountably popular all over the country. There was no more macho drink to be swigging in the Students' Union in the 1970s than Newkie Brown, straight from the clear glass bottle. By 1997, Scottish and Newcastle Breweries were claiming that it was the most widely distributed alcoholic drink on the market. There are dozens of better bottled beers now, from micro-breweries in and around Newcastle, as well as everywhere else in the country. As for Broon, it is now brewed at John Smiths in Tadcaster, it retains its popularity with bikers and vast quantities are exported to the United States without ever seeing Newcastle.

As I was writing this, in fact, news came through that brown was going to become a lot less brown than it was. It is going to be several shades lighter, because the health conscious Americans mistrust the amount of caramel in it. Forgive me if you are an aficionado, but that explains that cloying aftertaste in the back of the throat.

I'm beginning to wonder whether I'll ever see Newcastle, when we go past Annfield Plain again – I wouldn't want to wrestle with Annfield Complicated – do a couple of laps of the well-heeled suburb of Whickham and pick up and drop off at the Metro Centre. It is after leaving that particular Temple to Mammon that you begin to see what it is about Newcastle upon Tyne that excites such loyalty and fervour. There is no city in Britain where you make such a spectacular entrance by road or rail, although Edinburgh comes close. Crossing the Tyne by any one of its multifarious bridges still feels like you're arriving somewhere significant.

On the Newcastle bank of the Tyne, my favourite vantage point is the roof garden of the Bridge Hotel – a pub which, incidentally, claims to have the oldest continuously running folk club in the country. From the garden, you can see all the comings and goings on the bridges. Newcastle United fans used to gather here and chant 'Shearer, Shearer.' Possibly they still do, given how reluctant Geordies are to let go of their legends. Away fans used to spot their confreres arriving by coach and reply with 'Shearings, Shearings.'

All seven of Newcastle's bridges connect it with Gateshead, the little brother on the south bank of the Tyne. On the face of it, you would travel a long way to find a better candidate to be swallowed up by its neighbour. But Gateshead has been fighting back. The Sage, one of the country's best performing venues, is in Gateshead. So is the contemporary art gallery, The Baltic. Daniel Defoe wrote *Robinson Crusoe* in Gateshead; in Newcastle, not a word. The Angel of the North is South of the river, in Gateshead. So is the Metro Centre and the International Stadium, home until recently to the region's semi-professional rugby league club – which has now admittedly been rebranded as Newcastle Thunder – as well as athletics.

That was along with, until 2008, one of the symbols of Newcastle's renowned nightlife, the floating night-club, The Tuxedo Princess. The former car ferry on the Stranraer-Larne route was originally meant to be moored on the Newcastle side, but after being blocked by planning objections, set up shop instead under the Tyne Bridge in Gateshead in 1983. The turntable which spun lorries around, enabling them to drive off the way they had driven on, became a revolving dance floor, well known for its disorientating effect on those who had enjoyed a typical Geordie night out.

Newcastle might once have been world famous for sending its coal far and wide; now it is renowned primarily for its nightlife. The area around the Bigg Market is the epicentre of it all and there's no doubt about it, the Geordies really do love a night out. You can tell it's winter, because they put a vest on; nothing else, just a vest. As they never tire of reminding the rest of us, they are a hardy bunch. Even the owner of Newcastle United, Mike Ashley, follows the unwritten law by going to matches in the winter in shirt-sleeves. Mind you, he looks as though he might well have a couple of quilted jackets on underneath.

Another point in the Geordies' favour is that a night out in Newcastle is not usually an aggressive experience. Compared with other cities and considering how many drunk people there are in circulation, there is relatively little violence. Of course, now that I've written that, I will inevitably get my head kicked in the next time I go there. The last time I sampled the atmosphere was when I was booked to speak at the Newcastle University Rugby League Club annual dinner; Why Aye – all the glamorous gigs. Due to a slight administrative error, I turned up a day early, so I had a bit of time to kill. Part of the solution was to catch a bus to South Shields, cross the Tyne on the ferry and come back into the city via North Shields.

Both Shields are places where you suddenly feel a lot closer to continental Europe than you do to Lancashire. The sense of 'otherness' is intensified by the way that most people are speaking in tongues. Surveys by call centres have suggested that Geordie is the accent most victims prefer to hear when they are cold-called. That doesn't mean, I suspect, that they understand it all that well; they just rather like the sound of it. Take the universal Geordieism, for instance: Why Aye. For starters, is it a question or a statement? Does it mean yes or no? Or is it suspended somewhere in between? Is it a bit like 'si' in French, when it is used to mean 'oh, yes it does.' Or is it more like a sceptical 'you don't say'?

It gets used for 'hullo' and 'goodbye'. Like Chinese, it is heavily reliant on the tone employed, taking on an entirely different meaning if you pitch it wrongly. Like the French 'ça va', you can use it to fill in the gaps in a conversation, like linguistic putty.

Why Aye; Newcastle bus station is right in the middle of the Toon. I've got itchy feet, though; maybe something to do with a policy decision to start wearing socks again. It was in Lincoln that I succumbed, as soon as a telltale East Coast chill started to nibble at my toe-ends. I went into Primark prepared to be shocked by the price of such a basic commodity. In a sense, I was, because the robbing retailers wanted a whole £2 for five pairs. I know they must be made in a part of the world where wages are low, but how, short of slave labour, can they flog them for 40p a pair, 20p a sock. It's so ridiculous that they come with a twinge of guilt attached to them. I want to ask the girl on the checkout whether I can pay a little more and sink a well or build a primary school in the sock-knitters' village, just to even things up a bit.

A few days later, I'm revelling in the Joy of Sox in Newcastle bus station, but not ready to stop for the night, so I hop aboard one ready to depart for Hexham, having checked that it is in approximately the right direction. You could argue that the correct direction would be north to Berwick-upon-Tweed, the English town with the football club in the Scottish league. The trouble with that is that I would have to come back to Newcastle, because any cross-country route from Berwick would take me over the Scottish border and out of the scope of my magic piece of plastic.

The one surprise in Newcastle is that there are a few people not eating. According to a survey released shortly after this jaunt, the North East dominates the national league tables for obesity by greedily filling the top eight places, with County Durham the best of the best. That pease pudding has a lot to answer for. But, of course, it is the best pease pudding in the world, just like the Brown Ale and the football.

YOU really can't beat the feeling of arriving in a strange town, with no real idea of where you're going to stay or what you're going to do. Better still when it involves arriving in a strange county, of which you have barely heard and which almost nobody knows exists – or existed.

That is the situation in Hexham, not merely a small

165

town on the road between Newcastle and Carlisle, but also the historic centre of Hexhamshire. In one sense, I had less excuse than most for my ignorance on the subject, because there are at least two songs I know which locate themselves very specifically in Hexhamshire. I suppose I thought it must be made up, like Borsetshire or Greater Manchester. On the contrary, it is the very real remnant of centuries-old political power struggles in the North East.

Although it is planted firmly in rural Northumberland, Hexhamshire has only been a part of it since 1837. Before that, it was an enclave of royal land set amongst vast acres controlled by the Prince Bishops of Durham. At various times, it was referred to as the Liberty, the Regality or the Peculiar of Hexhamshire. It must have been difficult to work out who was collecting your dustbins at any given time. There were similar arrangements affecting Allertonshire (around Northallerton), Richmondshire, in North Yorkshire, and even Hullshire – which definitely sounds fictional and adds a whole new dimension to the great Humberside identity debate. Elsewhere in the country, there is Hallamshire, which covers Sheffield and much of South Yorkshire, and Winchcombeshire, in the Cotswolds. There's no point campaigning for Home Rule for Hexhamshire, because, in a sense, they have already had it.

All these considerations were subordinate, this particular, or Peculiar night, to the question of whether there was a bed to be had in Hexham. As befits a place with its tangled history, there was a distinctive system in place. A pub on the main street didn't have rooms itself, but it had a list of phone numbers for everywhere that did, just in case the information was needed. This is where information meets altruism. Better still, when my phone ran out of gas minutes after arriving in Hexham, they invited me to use the pub's landline. In other words, they were about a million times more helpful than any number of official bureaux around the country. I bet they could have given me the full run-down on what you have to do to attain Shire status and sung me a few verses of 'The Hexhamshire Lass' if I had asked them to.

> 'Hey for the thick and the thin.
> Hey for the muck and the mire.
> I want to see my lass,
> Who lives in Hexhamshire.'

I doubt, however, whether they could have helped me with another puzzle of English place-naming – the number of locations which call themselves 'Isles' but which are really nothing of the sort. This is essentially a Southern problem. On this route, or not far from it, I had come across the Isle of Purbeck, the Isle of Portland, the Isle of Thanet, the Isle of Sheppey and the Isle of Grain, all of which seem to be pretty securely joined to the mainland. You could make out a case for the Isle of Dogs and for the indisputably land-locked Isle of Ely. That is so-named because it was once surrounded by fens and marshes. Purbeck in Dorset is a peninsular rather than an island. Portland is joined to the mainland at low tide. Sheppey and Grain – where Boris Johnson wanted to build the new London Airport – are reclaimed from the mudflats of the Thames estuary by man-made barriers. Thanet is basically north-east Kent. Complicated place, the coast of England.

Whilst I'm musing on this over a pint of Hexhamshire ale, the barmaid has found me a room at a bed and breakfast just a short walk out of town. As soon as the door opens, I know it is going to be somewhat unusual. The hallway and downstairs rooms are so crammed with copper and brass that they give off a warm, metallic glow. The landlady herself looks like she has been chiselled out of bronze. All the way up the stairs and into the guest rooms, the walls are covered with china plates, every shelf and flat surface with other assorted ceramics and there is another area devoted to African musical instruments. It's going to be like sleeping in an over-stocked museum, a bit reminiscent of that one in the film. Everything is in such immaculate order that it speaks of a relentless regime of dusting and polishing, with little time for any other hobbies. But then I spot the well-stocked – and inevitably ornate and gleaming – drinks cabinet. Out front, in the positions of honour, are four ornate blown glass tumblers, of the type normally associated with the Venetian island of Murano and marked as follows: Sober, Pissed, Drunk and Shit-Faced. They sit uncomfortably with a stern notice warning guests not to stagger back intoxicated and rowdy from town.

I never meet the man of the house, but I can hear him beavering away out the back. I can also imagine a nightly ritual.

'Guests all back?'

'Yes, dear.'

'Brasses all polished?'

'Yes, dear.'

'Very well then, let's get shit-faced.'

I'm so pleased with my digs that I feel a sort of moral obligation to go back to the pub that found them for me when I arrived friendless in an unheard-of county. But the band advertised to appear that night was a Deep Purple tribute act and gratitude only stretches so far. Actually, it was worse than that, because the promise was of a particular LP, *Deep Purple in Rock*, reproduced track-by-track in the original order, which elevates this sort of follow-my-leader routine to an heroic status. Actually, that could be the name of a tribute act. This Saturday – Live on Stage – Heroic Status Sing the Songs of Rossi and Parfitt. I opt instead for a backstreet pub called The Tannery – a reference to the leather working that used to be Hexham's main industry. It's one of the best nights of the whole expedition. Not only is the food and drink thoroughly canny – a range of local beers and plaice goujons cooked Mexican-style in tortillas – but there's a band on who aren't trying to be Deep Purple.

I thought at first that they were called the Cute Jumpers, but the young girl fan who turns out to be the daughter of the harmonica player is actually saying the Q Jumpers, which is a lot better. They don't quite play blues and they don't quite play rockabilly, so they quite logically call it bluesabilly. They are hot-foot from playing to 2,000 in a marquee at a bikers' festival, which I gather was a bit of a triumph. Half a dozen new fans have followed them from there, then there's the gob-iron man's daughter and me, until the music starts to bring others in.

These are men who take their music seriously. After one well-received number, harmonica turns to the guitar/ singer and mutters: 'Why aye! Don't you EVER do that to me again!' After the next song, the singer growls between clenched teeth: 'And why aye! Don't you do THAT to me!' They offer each other the chance to go outside and sort out who has done what to whom.

'Are they always like this?' I ask the daughter.

'Why aye!' she says. 'They're usually worse.'

After taking great care not to inadvertently become shit-faced, I buy a new phone charger in the morning from the landlady to replace the one I've lost; there's probably a room full of them in display cabinets somewhere on the premises.

Route 63

You can catch a bus from Hexham to Hadrian's Wall, but I've had my statutory glimpses of it, not to mention walking the length of the damn thing a few years back. And the alternative is just too tempting. Every so often on a trip like this, you come across a link in the chain that is just too good to be true. Investigating Hexham bus station – a pull-in off the main street – the previous evening, I had discovered that there was one bus a day to Keswick; actually all the way from Newcastle to Keswick, which, at 82 miles, is one heck of a bus ride for nothing.

Going to meet my baker

THE 888 bus route through the North Pennines has been called the most beautiful in Britain; a big claim but one with which I wouldn't necessarily argue, although there are some stretches of the South Coast and the far South West that would run it close.

It has also been bracketed with journeys through the Rockies as among the most spectacular in the world; again, you'll get no argument from me. It's a summer-only route and we owe it to Wright Brothers Coaches of Alston – not to be confused, I presume, with the flight pioneers, Wilbur and Orville Wright, although the bus they use on the Newcastle-Keswick run is of a similar vintage.

My nearest bus stop is outside the police station and the 888 is sufficiently late to plant a seed of doubt about its existence. But then there it is, chugging around the corner from the town centre and very definitely a coach in appearance. This is one of those services which, if you were to follow North Devon's example, you could get away with excluding from the scope of the free bus pass. There is no such meanness of spirit in Northumberland, however, nor in Cumberland, nor even in the Regality of Hexhamshire. I've settled for that version of its historic title because the Northumbrian songwriter, Terry Conway, called his paean to the area 'Fareweel Regality'. The best-known version of it is by The Unthanks and I hear it in my mind's ear – well, if the mind has an eye, why not an ear as well? – as we climb up and away from the town.

> 'And there's naught that I can bid you,
> But that peace and love gan with you,
> Never mind wherever call the fates,
> Away from Hexhamshire.'

We're heading for Alston, which boasts proudly of its status as England's highest market town. It doesn't hold a regular market any more, but it could if it wanted to, which is always nice to know. It was also once the prime area in the country for mining silver. It is notable now for a survey in 2005, which proclaimed that it was more deficient in female inhabitants than any town in Britain; a ratio of one-to-ten was mentioned, which must make the barn dances interesting. A campaign was started to persuade young women to relocate to Alston, but with only very limited success.

We almost add to Alston's unwanted statistics. Rounding one of the bends leading down towards the town, I look up and see, coming towards us on our side of the road, a Warburtons bread van. It was not so much a moment in which your past life flashes before you; more of a brisk jog through bread-related memories. Warburtons were always the big, bad guys as far as we were concerned; my dad worked for the opposition bakery, Price's, and Warby's products were not allowed in the house. Price's never learnt the art of self-promotion and were eventually gobbled up by the North East outfit Greggs, effectively putting my dad out of work, at least for the two days it took him to find another job. Warburtons, by contrast, went on to rule the world, trading on a bogus northernness – all brass bands and cobbles – that convinced the public that they were getting something baked with loving, individual attention by cheerful Boltonians. The greatest thing since sliced bread, in fact, which some people think Warby's invented. Every time one of their adverts came on the telly, he would harrumph. He will no doubt be scandalised by the new campaign that features Sylvester Stallone bounding, *Rocky*-style, up the steps of Bolton Town Hall, brandishing a large, sliced white loaf. I once found him in the kitchen at my house, looking disapprovingly at the breadbin and some Warburtons oven-bottom barms which had somehow sneaked in there.

All in all, it would have been just too thickly spread with irony for me to be killed – or maybe just maimed – by a Warby's wagon. The driver didn't much fancy it either and somehow managed to heave our ageing coach over to the other side of the road and get us through unscathed. Remarkably, given Alston's gender imbalance, the driver was a young woman, about 5ft tall, but brawny around the shoulders and arms. Good job, really. I've already registered my admiration for the driving skills and sheer physical strength of country bus drivers, but this was above and beyond the call of duty. Had she been watching the spectacular scenery, I don't think all of us would be here to tell the tale. We had a 20 minute break at Alston; to compose ourselves, I thought, maybe with a spot of counselling thrown in, but apparently they have a rest stop there every day, whether they have recently cheated death or not.

After that the journey was what you might call uneventful by comparison, although the views remained awe-inspiring. The A686 crosses the cherished Settle-Carlisle rail line at Langwathby and it's on to Penrith, another of those towns whose main reason for being there is as a gateway to somewhere else; in this case, The Lakes.

THE Lake District is so synonymous these days with fresh air and fun that it comes as a shock to find that the visitors in the 18th century, many of whom were fascinated by the place, also regarded it with a certain amount of dread and awe.

It was not seen as a cosy, welcoming environment, but rather as a hostile and threatening one. Daniel Defoe – he of *Robinson Crusoe* fame – described it in fairly typical terms when he visited in 1724 for his *Tour Thro' the Whole Island of Great Britain*. He called the Lakeland landscape 'the wildest, most barren and frightful that I have passed in England.'

Its current image around the world, on the other hand, is stuck somewhere in between William Wordsworth and Beatrix Potter, a mixture of daffodils and fluffy bunnies. The prettification of the Lake District can be said to begin with Wordsworth's early poems, although he probably failed to realise that every time he picked up his quill pen he was cranking up the price of Lakeland cottages 200 years later by a few more quid.

Like a few other places in this book, the Lakes are a bit of a con. If you see a well-maintained hamlet, the chances are that it has been tastefully restored for holiday lets or second homes. It is almost impossible to earn enough money in the Lakes to enable you to live there. It's as uninhabitable as it was in Defoe's day, but for a different reason. It could be straight from the pages of *Catch 22*. Another conundrum about the Lakes, by the way. There are a lot more of them than you think – and a lot less. There are 21 lake-sized bodies of water, but only one of them, Bassenthwaite, that has the word 'lake' in its name. The rest are Meres or Waters, like the two best known, Windermere and, just down the way from Keswick high street, Derwent Water.

Keswick is its usual, bustling self. Over the past couple of decades, numbers of one very specific type of tourist have gone through the roof. Go on just about any day of the year and you will find hordes of Japanese – mainly young girls, but not exclusively – pursuing the Beatrix Potter experience. Her 28 books about Peter Rabbit and company made her the world's best-selling children's author. She is as popular in Japan as sushi and karaoke and, wherever you go in Keswick, you will be tripping over diminutive Japanese, dragged down by the weight of boxed sets of books, souvenir pots and stuffed Jemima Puddleducks. It's a weird cultural transfer, because I doubt that Beatrix had the Japanese market in mind when she penned *The Tale of Peter Rabbit* and the rest of her canon. But then the *Hello Kitty* phenomenon has been equally potent in the opposite direction. I noticed the other day that you can buy a pink *Hello Kitty* assault rifle for the junior markswoman in your life, so there truly is no clash of cultures which can be completely ruled out.

I don't know whether the Japanese flock in great numbers to one of Keswick's other attractions, the Pencil Museum. I'm told that it's more interesting than it sounds, to which the only answer is that it better had be. I had made a note to visit it, but I rubbed it out. Other north-western museums which sound equally exciting are the hat museum in Stockport and the one in Southport devoted to the history of the lawnmower. In Keswick, the bus station almost counts as a tourist attraction in itself. It's attached to Booths supermarket and adjoins their open-air terrace café, where you can relax, eat good, local food and wait for your bus to arrive. When it does, the key is to get a seat upstairs for an unbeatable view of the Lake District. That includes travelling the length of Thirlmere, passing the village of Grasmere, where Wordsworth lived, and carrying on via Ambleside to Windermere. If you're lucky enough to have a dry day for it, it's another of the world's best bus rides. At Windermere, we're just a couple of miles away, across the lake by ferry, from Beatrix Potter's farm at Near Sawrey, which, in her day, was in Lancashire, as indeed was Windermere itself. The last time I was there, I took my grandchildren on a boat ride to Ambleside, which they seemed to enjoy as much as generations before have done. We especially liked it when, as we were waiting to board on the way back, the ferryman whipped out a mandolin, on which he practiced rather tentatively until it was time to cast off again.

It was a few miles before Windermere, though, that two people I will definitely remember got onto the bus. It took me a while to realise that they were a couple; well-dressed, in their mid-50s, I would think and, like Mr Jeremy Fisher or Mrs Tiggiwinkle, with a tale to tell, if they felt inclined. They took a double seat each, him behind and her in front and never exchanged a single word nor the slightest glance or gesture. How do I know they were together, then? Only from one moment, about an hour into the trip.

She got out a plastic container of grapes, ate half of them and, still without a word, passed the rest to him. He ate the remainder and, equally seamlessly and silently, passed the empty box back to her. I know you shouldn't try to psychoanalyse people from the way they eat grapes, but I found this pretty fascinating. I've narrowed it down to two possibilities. Either they really can't stand to have any dealings with each other and the grapes are just the residue of a broken relationship. Or, they know and understand each other so well that they don't need to speak, even when there is fruit to be divvied up.

Either way, I shall remember them as the absolute epitome of a nice, quiet bus ride. Buses can be notorious for slightly mad people engaging you in unhinged and unwanted conversation or just ranting on at the world in general – not a big problem for me on this trip, perhaps because they were busy avoiding me – but this was a timely illustration of the power of silence. I wonder, however, how they would have coped with a drama like the cliff-hanger on the previous bus. Would one of them have shouted out in panic? 'You spoke first,' the other would say triumphantly. 'You buy the grapes.' I never found out, because they got out on the outskirts of Lancaster, still with no signs of recognition passing between them. It was only then that I noticed a curious thing; everyone on the bus had fallen silent, as though the Quiet Couple of Cumbria had cast a spell over us.

THE brief I gave myself for this trip was quite clear; a circuit of England, sticking as closely as possible to the edge and eventually getting back to where I started.

If there is a point where I start to feel 'at home,' it should be where the bus tyres cross into the historic county of Lancashire. That is just a recipe for confusion, however, because Lancashire used to extend deep into the Lake District, as well as taking in the whole of the Furness peninsular, including Barrow and Walney Island – a genuine island, this one, and a feeling of being at the margin of the known world that is at least as strong as being at Land's End. The idea of this being in Lancashire makes no sense at all, until you think of Furness's historic land links with the rest of the world being via the sands of Morecambe Bay at low tide. After the tragedy of the Chinese cockle pickers in 2004, we are more conditioned than ever into regarding the sands as a death-trap. They obviously can be, but they were the way in and the way out for stagecoaches and the like.

Our stagecoach goes from Kendal, down the A6 to Lancaster. For an historic county town with a well-known name, it is a slightly low-key place, especially by comparison with the tourist magnet that is its natural rival, York. Lancaster won the Wars of the Roses; York won the War of the Credit Cards. It's a pleasant enough destination, with a couple of eye-catching structures and one of the country's more intriguingly named football grounds – The Giant Axe. The stadium, home to Lancaster City, apparently resembles the shape of a large battleaxe when seen from the air. I'll take their word for that.

Apart from Lancaster Castle, which for much of its life has doubled as a prison and a court – the Pendle Witches were tried here – the city has 'The Taj Mahal of the North' – The Ashton Memorial. There are points of similarity; it was built by the bereaved millionaire, Baron Ashton, in memory of his wife, and it is white. There are elements which echo St Paul's and St Peter's in Rome, so he can hardly be accused of lacking ambition. From its elevated position in Williamson

Park, near the spot where those condemned in trials at the castle were hung, it can be seen from miles around and for that alone justifies its other description of 'England's Grandest Folly.'

The idea of the folly – a decorative building of no practical use – is not uniquely English, but we do seem to have an awful lot of them. In fact, you would have your work cut out to ever be very far away from one. Headley and Meulenkamp in their seminal work, *Follies*, list 60 in Lancashire alone. They also reveal that only two citizens attended the official opening of the Ashton Memorial in 1909. It rained. They unhesitatingly nominate Brighton as England's most be-follied town, with the Royal Pavilion, where I took a nap several hundred bus-miles ago, spear-heading their claim. I was equally impressed, though, by the inclusion of a gothic gateway leading to a bowling green in Helston; about 30 yards from where I stayed in that fine little town. It's almost enough of a distinction to make up for the fact that it's a flat green, rather than the infinitely trickier crown green.

One thing this expedition has achieved is to vastly increase the number of places at which I can exclaim 'I've been there!' when they flash onto the early evening news. If we ever have another winter of floods and storms – which we will – I could very quickly become insufferable.

A few miles south of Lancaster, sandwiched between the A6 and the M6, is the city's university. It's a campus in the middle of nowhere, but, according to all the ranking tables, a major success. You can have a pub crawl on that campus, because each college has its own bar. I'm not saying that's the reason for its glowing reputation, but it can't hurt. The bus half-empties at the university gates and the feeling of being on the home stretch intensifies.

Preston succeeded Lancaster as Lancashire's administrative centre; a bigger place and more central in the county. I make a point of never missing Preston Guild, a celebration of all things Prestonian, but that cannot be described as a major commitment, because it only comes around every 20 years. It has even passed into the language, with 'Every Preston Guild' being synonymous with not very often. Preston got permission to stage an annual event to mark the permission given to merchants and tradesmen to operate in the town in 1179. In 1542, it was decided that the procession and the banqueting every year was a bit too much of a good thing, so they went to the opposite extreme of a 20-year timetable. They have had some big names there over the years; the famous tightrope walker, Blondin, did his stuff over Preston Marsh in 1807.

I have a bit of a balancing act of my own to perform, as well. I've reached the stage where I just want to get home, but I know there are people planning to meet me, with whom I can't communicate because I haven't been able to charge up my phone. I have to throw myself on the mercies of the roughest pub in Preston, which is deep in karaoke mode. All the plugs are in use, they tell me, above the din of 'I Will Survive' – or rather the rough pub version, 'I Will Survive If I Don't Look at Anyone the Wrong Way' – but I can piggy-back on a socket with a dodgy-looking adaptor. It's a tricky moment. One false move and some fairly formidable customers could be trying to sing along to the last thing I recorded on my phone, which is a chap in Kings Lynn talking about country bus services. It might take all of 20 years to be forgiven for such an error.

Eventually, all becomes clear. My bus guru, Andrew, is meeting me in Preston, anyone else at Mission Control at the Doffcocker Inn in Bolton. We catch the first available 125 to Chorley, which, appropriately, is a round-the-houses job through Bamber Bridge and Clayton Brook. From there we step straight onto another 125 to Bolton. I think I'm getting the hang of this.

DO you remember going on holiday as a child and seeing the familiar landmarks when you got back? If you had been lucky enough to have been away for a whole fortnight, it was almost like a look into a past life. That's what it was like at the scrag-end of the Big Free Bus Ride, passing Rivington Pike and the reservoir, with its own ambitious folly – a scale replica of the long-demolished Liverpool Castle.

Through Horwich and past Bob's Smithy; no actual smithy now, of course, but the pub that bore its name still going strong. For a variety of reasons, though, the journey has to end a mile or so further down the road at the Doffcocker. It's only fitting that a project which has been almost obsessively interested in the names that people give to places and things should end in a pub whose name is one of the hardest to explain. There is a theory that it has something to do with the cotton industry, but the general wisdom now is that it was built where a stream crossed the toll road and those walking that way had to remove their clogs – or doff their cockers – to negotiate it. Yes, I know, it doesn't sound very convincing to me either.

One extra complication is that it is known locally as The Big Cocker, as opposed to The Hope and Anchor across the road, which is always referred to as The Little Cocker. If

I was in search of curiosities, I could just as easily have stayed at home.

The (Big) Cocker is also a rare example of a 'calendar' pub, which makes it a bit of a folly in itself. When it was re-built to replace the thatched original, it was given four floors, for the seasons of the year; seven rooms on each floor, for the days of the week; 12 cellars – which seems a lot; 52 doors and 365 window panes. Little wonder that you can finish up there not knowing what day of the week it is.

From that I naturally exclude the Fenton brothers, Keith and Pete, who are the clean-up squad, responsible for making me presentable before I actually go home. And how are we to get there? Well, we could walk. We could get a bus from up the road, or a combination of buses, down the road and back up the other road. After four and a bit weeks on the buses, though, it should be obvious where my loyalties would lie.

Reader, I phoned a cab.

Diversion: Blackpool

AND that's that. Or it should be, except that I can't quite resist a quick side-trip to a town where I lived for a couple of years and which has a unique relationship with buses.

Blackpool was the one town in Britain that kept its trams as a local alternative, when everywhere else got rid of theirs. Or at least they kept them along the seafront; all the inland lines, of which there were a number, went on the Great Tram-Track to Extinction. Trams have now made a spirited comeback, in places like Manchester, Sheffield and Croydon. Naturally, they cherry-pick the most lucrative lines, but that leaves plenty of work for the humble omnibus to continue to do.

Getting to Blackpool by bus is no problem; the trusty 125 to Preston and frequent services to the coast from there. I plan to attack from the north, from the delectable fishing village of Fleetwood, but miss the connection and switch instead to a personal pincer movement, sneaking up on it from the south. That involves catching the bus that goes through Freckleton, Warton, Lytham and St Annes – the areas where all the money made in Backpool goes to. Freckleton is so uncompromisingly bypassed these days that it is decades since I'd been in the centre of the village. It's notable for the most immaculate war memorial of the whole route. Set in a manicured little garden, it looks as though someone has the job of polishing it twice a day. In view of that tell-tale hint of an idyllic England, I should have realised that, within a week, the local vicar, his wife and daughter would be in custody over the death of an infant. I should have guessed, but I didn't.

I don't know whether Freckleton suffered disproportionately in the two wars, but the next village, Warton, is one which, as the home of British Aerospace, is linked with just about any outbreak of hostilities, anywhere in the world.

One difference I notice on this route is the number of residential parks that have sprung up; what Americans would call trailer parks, but for which there is no equally vivid name in British English. I doubt whether many of the residents would settle for being known as Trailer Park Trash, which is how their transatlantic equivalents are dismissed.

Most people on the bus are going to Lytham, which seems a younger, livelier place than I remember from my time living on the Fylde Coast. Mind you, it is the end of November and there are customers sitting in the sunshine outside the numerous cafés drinking their lattes in their shirt-sleeves. It all feels like a bonus dished out to an already fortunate place, like a millionaire coming up on the Premium Bonds, which used to be drawn, by a computer named ERNIE, just down the road at St-Annes-on-Sea. My old colleague, Roy Edmonds, who has lived on the Coast for a big slice of his life, says that Lytham has 'taken off' over the last few years. Along with St Annes, it was, when I lived there briefly, synonymous with retirement and a dour, joyless gentility. St Annes Square now is full of the bustle of prosperity as well. The Fylde peninsula always was a particularly polarised place; viewed from the top deck of the number 68, that process seems to have galloped on apace.

The gap between St Annes and Starr Gate is notable for its sandhills. It's another of the spots on this itinerary that induces a little shudder, because I did several weeks of pre-season training with Blackpool Borough rugby league club here. Running up and down loose sand on a 45 degree gradient with another prop forward on my back is the hardest work I've ever done in my life. It was so hard that I couldn't be bothered going for a drink after training, which had them checking me for a pulse. When you start running on grass again, though, you feel like Superman. That raises the question of why every team doesn't do it. A few weeks into the season, we had our answer. We had nine players with hamstring injuries, as those muscles celebrated their new-found freedom by snapping like rotten rubber bands as soon as you put them under any strain.

Starr Gate marks the southern terminal of the Fylde Coast's celebrated tramways, or least it does now. From 1903 to 1937, though, they ran all the way to Lytham, which explains a little kiosk I noticed there, with 'Lytham Tramways' chiselled into its lintel.

Route 63

Where the trams from Blackpool turn around – or strictly speaking where, being double-ended, they don't have to turn around – we turn right towards another transport casualty, Squires Gate (later Blackpool) Airport. People had been taking to the skies there for 105 years when the airport closed in 2014. The famed aviatrix, Amy Johnson, made her last completed flight from Blackpool. I remember using it for flights to Belfast and the Isle of Man. The Belfast run was a daily contract to deliver the Irish editions of national newspapers to a sleeping city which, I couldn't help noticing from the air, was lit partly by orange street lights and partly by green ones. There were also the end-of-season flights to Spain that were generally known as the Landladies' Specials. Now it is deserted, although, like everything else that closes down in Blackpool, there have been plenty of rumours of it re-opening, which it did, at least for flights to Belfast and the Isle of Man, in April.

Still closed to you, however, unless you have your wristband, is Blackpool Pleasure Beach, which controversially introduced an entrance charge in 2009. Apparently, families were spending the day pottering around, watching the rides and eating picnics, committing the mortal Blackpool sin of not spending any money. The Big One, its giant rollercoaster, towers above everything in South Shore. As if to emphasise the contrast with Lytham St Annes, our route takes us round the back of the Pleasure Beach, not its best side. There are some of the most dispiriting small hotels, bed and breakfasts and holiday flats you could wish to see. On one corner, there is a half-collapsed shop held up by a sign reading 'Closing Down Sale.' For a moment, I misread it as 'Falling Down Sale.'

The New South Promenade is supposed to be a cut above all this, but then came the curious affair of the Broadway Hotel.

From the outside, it doesn't look like the worst place in Blackpool, but when a couple from Cumbria stayed there in August 2014 they described it in their online review as a 'filthy dirty rotten stinking hovel.' Yes, but did they like it or not? Hard to say. You used to get entries in visitors' books in the old days along the lines of: 'A filthy dirty rotten stinking hovel. Thanks for everything. See you next year.'

What the modern guests definitely didn't like was being charged an extra £100 on their credit card for infringing the hotel's 'no bad reviews' policy. Not surprisingly, they went to the papers and, for a while, the Broadway was the world's most notorious hotel, edging out Fawlty Towers and the Bates Motel. Among the mouthwatering details that emerged were a pair of sweaty socks abandoned in a room and staff serving breakfast whilst drinking cans of Strongbow; a truly authentic Blackpudlian touch there. For your information – it costs £36 for a double and reservations are not always necessary.

There are some more conventional icons in Blackpool. I recall once flying home from somewhere in the world and, bleary-eyed and with no idea where I was, looking out of the window and seeing three piers thrusting out into the sea. That can only be Blackpool. Whether you are travelling by plane, tram or bus, the other landmark stands out equally strongly, just to the south of the third of those piers. Headley and Meulenkamp classify Blackpool Tower as a folly, but there, with all due respect to their expertise, I have to part company from them. It doesn't meet their own criterion of having no practical purpose. From its construction in 1894 to the present day, it has been devoted to the most practical purpose of all – making money.

Blackpool's is part of a short-lived craze for mini-Eiffel Towers around the turn of the 19th century. There were similar projects at Wembley and Morecambe and on the Isle of Man, but none of them amounted to much. New Brighton did rather better, its tower lasting until 1919. The one with real staying power, however, has been Blackpool. Roughly half the height of the Parisian prototype, it contains the Tower Ballroom and the Tower Circus, whose elephants were often exercising in single file along the Promenade as I arrived for work. You could work in Mumbai and not be able to boast of that. It was a suitably exotic preparation for what the day might bring.

The first story I was ever sent out on at *The West Lancashire Evening Gazette* involved a lion going missing from the Circus. It was only when I got there that it became apparent that it was a model lion, made not of fur but of fibreglass. As young Albert Ramsbottom found out in Stanley Holloway's monologue, 'Albert and the Lion,' however, there were once real ones there too. The Ballroom will be forever associated with Reginald Dixon and his mighty Wurlitzer organ, but its continued resonance as a mythic, romantic location was emphasised recently by Roy and Hayley dancing there to celebrate her impending decline and death in *Coronation Street*.

Just after the Tower, the bus turns inland opposite the North Pier. Credit where it's due, Blackpool has done its best with the Prom. With arty lighting and points of interest like the Comedy Carpet, a granite floor devoted to quotations from comedians, many of them with Blackpool connections, it has more appeal than it ever had. It also triggers some bizarre memories. When I worked on a bread van – not, repeat NOT a Warburtons one – delivering to Blackpool, we were too early one Saturday morning and parked up on the Prom for a fag. Within seconds there was a tap on the window and a strangely familiar voice asking if we had one to spare. It was a dishevelled Tommy Cooper. Only in Blackpool...

It's time to hop off this bus, cross the road and hop on the number 1 to Fleetwood, passing the landmark pubs – The Gynn, Uncle Tom's Cabin, with its own lift down to the beach. I would normally do this journey by tram, preferably an open-topped double-decker of the type that always recalls for me the streets of Hong Kong. I'm told by my research department that my belief that old ones from the Fylde Coast had a second life east of Suez is an urban myth, which seems a shame. Blackpool, aware as ever of what the market will stand, doesn't accept free passes on board them. Besides, the resort now has a brand new fleet of shiny purple trams, which look as though they could dash from Starr Gate to Fleetwood Ferry Pier in a couple of minutes. For much of the route to the north of Blackpool, the tram and bus run alongside each other, and, but for the driver sportingly stopping a few times to let the tram catch up, the bus is rather faster. Rossall School, that most windswept of private educational establishments, which still plays its unique version of hockey on the sands, has a stop of its own and, not long after that, we're in Fleetwood.

You wouldn't know it from the vantage point of a bus, but this place has a unique claim to fame as the first modern planned town in Britain. You would need to get at least as high as the top of one of its landlocked lighthouses to appreciate that. The bus terminates at the Pharos – to give the tallest of the lighthouses its Sunday name – not far from the North Euston Hotel, the very name of which is evidence that not all plans work out. The vision was that the West Coast Main Line of its day would go to Fleetwood, where passengers would switch from the train to the steamer that would take them the rest of the way to Scotland. It was a good plan, but only for the few years until a more direct route was carved out over Shap Fell.

The other part of the plan was fish, but, since Britain lost the Cod War, there has been less and less of that coming ashore at Fleetwood. Old school trawler skippers, the sort who used to have vodka on their cornflakes for breakfast, are turning in their graves. By a splendid irony, the one really thriving industry in Fleetwood recycles those days in edible form. Fisherman's Friends – the fiery lozenge, not to be confused with the previously mentioned shanty singers in Cornwall – have swept the world. Like Peter Rabbit, they are particularly popular in Japan. In fact, take any product that seems to have no possible relevance to Japan and the chances are that it will be wildly popular there.

The only other way in which the balance of power has swung north on the Fylde Coast is through football. Fleetwood Town, barely the standard of a village team when I lived in these parts, have strode into the Football League and, the way things are going, could overtake a chaotic Blackpool, still reeling on the rebound from their one, unlikely year in the Premier League, anytime now.

Whether you arrive by bus, tram or on foot, Fleetwood has that Ends of the Earth vibe that I find so seductive. There is, though, a further extreme to be explored here, one that tells a rather different story. Welcome to the future. Welcome to the Knott End Ferry.

I remember it as a sure and certain way of getting away from it all. Now it has rather more bustle about it than Fleetwood. All I can recall being there was a jetty, a pub and a few cottages. Now there is a café/restaurant, a golf club, a small housing estate and a quayside big enough to accommodate the Titanic – although depth of water could be a problem. Overlooking it all when it is finished will be a block of luxury flats that is taking shape on the harbourside. No matter that it will eventually be a candidate for Biggest Eyesore on the Fylde Coast – a hotly-disputed title if ever there was one – it marks a sea-change for the area. There's so much going on that in future Knott Enders will have to set sail for Fleetwood and Blackpool if they want a bit of peace and quiet. Don't worry about the name that inhabitants carry with them, by the way. It could be a lot worse if they lived on a hillock beside the defunct Bolton and Bury Canal. Imagine having to admit to the world that you are a Knob Ender.

The ferry has taken on a new seriousness. Not only does it charge you £1.50 each way for the five-minute voyage - £1 for concessions as I found out later – damn! It also has rules about what you can and can't do on board.

'You can't be eating that on here,' says the senior ferryman, gesturing at the bacon barm I'd bought before embarkation. Fortunately, there was no rule against carrying it over to Knott End and consuming it there. Not that I really needed it, not now that there is such a dizzying choice of food outlets. In the old days, you wouldn't have risked it without a couple of days' supplies.

Coming back on the ferry through the sunset – the alternative is a detour of several miles around the Wyre estuary – I get straight onto a Blackpool bus. This is not, however, the relatively direct route on which I arrived. This explores the backroads of the Fylde, through places like Carleton and Thornton, narrowly avoiding Poulton-le-Fylde and sneaking into Blackpool by the back door. One way and another, I had quite a time when I lived here. Another bus along Whitegate Drive takes me to the Saddle Inn and a reunion with a few other survivors of those days. Strictly speaking, we're not in Blackpool any more, but in the long-since swallowed up village of Great Marton, which was here when Blackpool was literally a murky pool on a barren foreshore.

The presence of Roy, who lives just around the corner, when he's not living in The Saddle, which is arguably the only unspoiled pub in the area, reminds me of a bus related incident in which we both played a part.

We were both working in Hong Kong at the time, him as a bedazzled newcomer, me as a gnarled veteran of a year or so and a font of local knowledge. The best way to get to the *South China Morning Post* in Quarry Bay was on one of the colony's vast fleet of mini-buses. They had no designated stops, so when you wanted to get off you simply shouted something that sounded like 'Yow Law!' Unfortunately, Cantonese is a tonal language and, if you say the same thing with a slightly different intonation, it means something else altogether. What Roy shouted was apparently so obscene that even the colorfully cursing and cheerfully profane Cantonese were shocked into silence. The bus screeched to a halt and Roy was ordered off pretty close to where he wanted to be. Local knowledge; it's a wonderful thing.

No such problems on the bus to Preston, which picks me up outside The Saddle, although outside Kirkham there is what appears to be the aftermath of a nasty accident, with a car halfway through a fence and plenty of flashing blue lights. Everybody, on and off the bus, pays it so little attention that I'm forced to the conclusion that it isn't real, but some sort of mock-up needed for some reason. Fantasy overlapping with reality; it was a feeling I often had in Blackpool, from the runaway lion onwards.

On the final, final bus, from Preston to Bolton, I run into two mates from the cricket club, on their way home from an evening in the fleshpots of Horwich. Jack is a veteran farmer, a tall, skinny livewire of a bloke, just recovering from a course of chemotherapy; Craig is a retired geology teacher, who has taken it upon himself to get Jack out and about between treatments. Both of them are using their bus passes, I have to confess, in a more constructive way than me.

'Have you been far?' they ask me. Well there, gents, I think I might have you beaten.

Fare Conclusions?

SO what have I got out of it, apart from cramps in the buttocks? Well, one of the great travel bargains of all time, for starters. And a completely different view of the country where I have spent most of my 63 years.

By travelling, roughly speaking, around its margins – its coasts and borders – I've been like an outsider looking in. The fact that the journey came just a few months after the most extreme and damaging winter in living memory meant that I saw England in recovery mode, shrugging off its local disasters.

Concurrent with that, the journey came as England was tying itself in knots over the issue of immigration. If it wasn't the elements threatening to submerge us, it was, it seemed, the East Europeans. As a counter-balance to this metaphor of England as an over-crowded life-boat, which will surely sink if another person climbs aboard, the view I got was of a country which was not only green, but for the most part, empty. That was not the vision of the United Kingdom Independence Party, whose rising vote in by-elections was the big political story of 2014. The *Times* made the UKIP leader, Nigel Farage, their Briton of the Year, supposedly 80 years to the day after they bestowed a similar honour on Oswald Mosley. Any belfries not already filled with the sounds of warning bells being rung before this astounding co-incidence surely must have been chiming lustily afterwards.

The trouble is that it's not true. The *Times* only introduced its Briton of the Year award a few years ago and has certainly never given it to Mosley. Could there be some confusion here with *Time* magazine, which has nominated its Man of the Year (now Person of the Year) since 1927, when the aviator, Charles Lindbergh, was the inaugural recipient? No sign of Sir Oswald in their list of winners since then. Their choice in 1934 was the American president, Franklin Delano Roosevelt, although they did give it to Hitler in 1938, but not, I think, with any sort of approbation.

I'm not so naïve as to think that the empty acres are the total answer to all the issues that UKIP stirs up. By and large, newcomers to this country want to live in towns and cities with jobs, infrastructure and, preferably, some of their fellow countrymen. In large swathes of the East of England that is changing the make-up of the population quite radically, but, if we don't like that, it is not for the bogus reason that the country is 'full', but for other deeper and darker reasons.

Besides, the majority of people who come to this country from abroad are only swimming with the economic tide. As I write, the latest examples are Portuguese bricklayers, who are apparently being brought in, at £200 a day, because there are no qualified English brickies. But, if that is the case, who is to blame, if 'blame' is even necessary? The predatory Portuguese, lining up in Lisbon and waiting for a chance to steal 'our' jobs? Shiftless Brits, who couldn't be bothered learning a useful skill? Or successive governments, who gave up building affordable housing where bricklayers could have served apprenticeships and learned their trade?

Far from depressing local wages, which is the charge normally flung at immigrant workers, the Portuguese brickies are apparently getting twice the usual rate. The same obviously doesn't apply to agricultural workers from Eastern Europe, who labour for what we would regard as an insulting pittance in the fields of Eastern England.

One thing I know is that if people glimpse the prospect of a better life on the other side of a border – let alone those fearing for their own lives if they stay put – you can't build a fence high enough to keep them out. That's something I could have had confirmed for me on the shores of Sicily or Lampadusa, the banks of the Rio Grande, or the Torres Strait islands to the north of Australia, but which was just as clear around The Wash.

The other thing that people told me I would find on this journey was an England where everywhere was growing more and more like everywhere else.

If you did a tour of out-of-town shopping centres and some High Streets, you would have no difficulty in believing this to be true. After all, England is a tiny country – you can get a bus around it, for heaven's sake; how much diversity can you cram into it? The refreshing answer which this journey suggested to me was: Quite a bit.

Maybe I was guilty of consciously seeking out places of character. I don't think so; I think it was a fair cross-section of urban and rural, prosperous and struggling, ancient and modern. It was how they came out on the map, at any rate. Of course, it could, by its very nature, only be a series of snatched snapshots, rather than an in-depth documentary about England and the English. There is a long and honorable tradition, however, of taking a head-long dash around a country as a way of getting to know it, including the likes of JB Priestley and working down from there. Perhaps it works well because it accentuates the contrasts.

For instance, you can have breakfast in Whitby, pease pudding in Newcastle and Cumberland sausage in Keswick, all on the same day. You'll have indigestion and be sick of the sight of buses, but it can be done. And you will certainly notice the differences.

After a thousand or so years – thank you, William the Bastard – as a unified entity, we still barely speak the same language. We don't sound the same; we don't even look the same. Throw in the continuing absorption of people from across the Channel and you have a country which is not full, but which is full of variety. Quirks and eccentricities are everywhere. You don't have to go looking for them; they come and find you.

I have a particular interest in the future of the English pub. That is, if it has a future – or even a present – which some commentators query. Sure, I saw plenty of public houses boarded up on my travels, but some of the great survivors, like the Bridge in Topsham or the Blue Anchor in Helston, more than make up for that. By contrast, some of the most vibrant and interesting new places to drink are micro-pubs, which have popped up in unlikely locations like Bolton and Manchester Markets. It was Hilaire Belloc who advised:

'When you have lost your pubs, drown your empty selves, for you will have lost the last of England.' We are some way from having to do that.

Then there are the hundreds of small breweries, some of them little more than a man in a shed, supposedly on their way to extinction not long ago, but now often brewing better beer – and cheaper – than the multi-nationals, with all their economies of scale and million dollar advertising or brainwashing budgets. Compared with 20 years ago, your chances of finding something distinctively local to drink are vastly enhanced just about anywhere in England. It's a wonderful example of an industry which has gone in precisely the opposite direction from the one all the experts predicted. Experts – what do they know?

I don't really do shops, but any country that boasts Boggis Electrical in Wrentham, Peter Scott's shoe emporium in Woodhall Spa and the extra-thin pipe-cleaner and rose-petal confetti stockists in Helston remains not only a Nation of Shopkeepers, but one with plenty of individual personality still intact. Okay, so Boggis Electrical has closed down, pulled the plug, as it were; I didn't say things were perfect.

There is still, though, a complex, intricate cultural map demarcating local differences. There might be a National Curriculum, but, almost without exception, any writer you would want on it has a strong sense of a particular place underlying his work.

What's more, it's a place you can get to by bus, for free if you're old or knackered enough. I call that a minor miracle.

If I was shocked by anything on my lap of England, it was not that it is swamped by in-comers nor that it has lost all its distinguishing features. It was how physically fragile it looked, even in the relatively benign summer months. On more than one section of the trip, I felt relieved to be seeing the landscape before it collapsed, or before I did. Submerge the Severn Valley, the Thames Valley and the Somerset Levels again, keep chipping away at the Jurassic Coast and equally crumbly Cleveland and North Yorkshire and there might not be much left.

That, however, reckons without the remarkable resilience of this land and of much that is in it. Perhaps the solution, though, is for every would-be immigrant to have to bring a sturdy canvas sack of hard-core from their homeland with them. That is a symbolic act that would carry more meaning for the England that I saw than the high wire fence and the drawbridge.

THE END

Please take all your personal belongings with you

FACTFILE

Number of buses (*including diversions*)**:** 107
Total mileage: 1,899 miles
Longest journey: Exeter to Poole, 120 miles
(*journey broken at West Bay*).
Longest continuous: Hexham to Keswick, 75 miles
Shortest journey: 1 mile, Gloucester Bus Station
to Bristol Road
Quickest journey: Plymouth to Ivybridge,
11 miles in 15 minutes
Slowest journey: Bluewater Shopping Centre
to Woolwich, 11 miles in 3.5 hours
Total bus fare: Zero
Total cost (*including Knott End Ferry*)**:** £3
Accidents: Zero
Near misses: 1
Breakdowns: 1
Bus services discontinued since trip: 1

ROUTE 63 LOG BOOK

Warning: Many routes are subject to change or discontinuation. Check before you travel.

Heading South
Doffcocker - Bolton (*First 501*)
Bolton - Leigh (*First 582*)
Leigh - Warrington (*Network Warrington 19*)
Warrington - Daresbury - Mickle Trafford (*usually!*) - Chester (*Arriva X30*)
Chester - Whitchurch (*Helms of Eastham 41*)
Whitchurch - Shrewsbury (*Arriva 511*)
Shrewsbury - Church Stretton - Craven Arms - Ludlow (*Minsterley Motors 435*)
Ludlow - Hereford
(*Lugg Valley Travel 490, 492 ... Sunday Service now axed*)
Hereford - Ross-on-Wye - Solomon's Tump - Gloucester (*Stagecoach 33*)
Gloucester - Cirencester - Gloucester (*Pulhams 852*)
Gloucester - Cam (*Stagecoach 62*)
Cam - Thornbury (*Severnside 87*)
Thornbury - Bristol (*First 78*)
Bristol - Wells (*First 376*)
Wells - Taunton (*First 29*)
Taunton - Wellington - Tiverton (*First 22*)
Tiverton - Exmoor - Barnstaple (*Stagecoach 155*)

Barnstaple - East-the-Water - Bideford (*Stagecoach 21A*)
Bideford - Holsworthy (*Stagecoach 85*)
Holsworthy - Bude (*Stagecoach 6*)
Bude - Okehampton - Wadebridge (*Stagecoach 595*)
Wadebridge - Welcome - Padstow (*Plymouth Citybus 75*)
Padstow - Newquay (*First 556*)
Newquay - St.Columb Major - Truro (*First 93 94*)
Truro - Helston (*First 36*)
Helston - Marazion - Penzance (*First 2*)
Penzance - Land's End - Penzance (*First 10*)
Penzance - Truro (*First 18*)
Truro - St Austell - Bodmin (*First 27*)
Bodmin - Liskeard (*Plymouth Citybus 75*)
Liskeard - Plymouth (*Plymouth Citybus 593*)

Going North
Plymouth - Ivybridge (*Stagecoach X38*)
Ivybridge - Paignton (*Stagecoach GOLD*)
Paignton - Torquay (*Stagecoach 12, 22, 110*)
Torquay - Dawlish - Topsham (*Stagecoach X46, 57*)
Topsham - Exeter (*Stagecoach 57*)
Exeter - West Bay - Weymouth - Poole (*First X53*)
Poole - Bournemouth (*Yellow Buses 1C*)
Bournemouth - Lymington (*More Bus X1 X2*)
Lymington - Southampton (*Bluestar Bus 6*)
Southampton - Fareham (*First X4 X5*)
Fareham - Portsmouth (*First 3, X4*)
Portsmouth - Bognor Regis - Arundel - Littlehampton -
Hove - Brighton (*Stagecoach 700 in sections*)
Brighton - Rottingdean - Eastbourne (*Brighton & Hove 12*)
Eastbourne - Hastings (*Stagecoach 99*)
Hastings - Lydd - Dymchurch - Hythe - Dover
(*Stagecoach 100 101*)

Route 63

Dover - Canterbury (*Diamond/Stagecoach 15*)
Canterbury - Faversham (*Stagecoach 3*)
Faversham - Sittingbourne (*Arriva 333*)
Sittingbourne - Chatham (*Glider 327*)
Chatham - Bluewater (*Arriva 700 701*)
Bluewater - Plumstead - Woolwich Arsenal
(*Stagecoach London 96*)
Woolwich - North Woolwich (*Ferry/foot*)
North Woolwich - Stratford (*Stagecoach London 473*)
Stratford – Bethnal Green
Bethnal Green - Liverpool St - Blackfriars (*CT Plus 388*)
Blackfriars - Southwark - Elephant & Castle - Camberwell
Green - Brixton - Clapham Park (*London Central 45*)
Stratford - Ilford - Romford (*Stagecoach London 86*)
Romford - Brentwood (*Go Ahead London 498*)
Brentwood - Colchester (*First 351, 71*)
Colchester - Stratford St Mary - Ipswich
(*Carters Coaches 93 94*)
Ipswich - Wickham Market (*First 64*)
Wickham Market - Saxmundham (*First 64*)
Saxmundham - Halesworth (*Borderbus 521*)
Halesworth - Southwold (*Anglian Bus 88A*)
Southwold - Wangford - Wrentham - Great Yarmouth
(*Anglian Bus 61*)
Great Yarmouth - Norwich (*First X1*)
Norwich - Dereham - King's Lynn (*First X1*)
King's Lynn - Walpoles - Terringtons - Suttons - Spalding
(*Norfolk Green 505*)
Spalding - Boston (*Brylaine 113*)
Boston - Coningsby - Tattershall - Woodhall Spa - Lincoln
(*Brylaine 5*)
Lincoln - Scunthorpe (*Stagecoach 103*)
Scunthorpe - Humber Bridge - Hull (*Stagecoach 350*)

Hull - Hessle Park & Ride (*Stagecoach Park and Ride Hull*)
Hull - Beverley (*East Yorkshire 121, 246*)
Beverley - Driffield - Scarborough (*East Yorkshire 121*)
Scarborough - Robin Hood's Bay - Whitby (*Arriva X93*)
Whitby - Middlesbrough (*Arriva X93*)
Middlesbrough - Durham (*Arriva X12*)
Durham - Annfield Plain - Whickham - Metro Centre -
Newcastle upon Tyne (*Go North East 44*)
Newcastle upon Tyne - Hexham (*Arriva 85*)
Hexham - Alston - Keswick (*Wright Bros 888*)
Keswick - Grasmere - Windermere - Lancaster
(*Stagecoach 555*)
Lancaster - Preston (*Stagecoach 40,41*)
Preston - Bamber Bridge - Chorley (*Stagecoach 125*)
Chorley - Doffcocker Inn (*Stagecoach 125*)
Bolton - Preston (*Stagecoach 125*)
Preston - Freckleton - Lytham St Annes - Blackpool
(*Stagecoach 68*)
Blackpool - Fleetwood (*Blackpool Transport 1*)
Knott End – Thornton - Carleton - Blackpool
(*Blackpool Transport 2C*)
Blackpool - Kirkham - Preston (*Stagecoach 61*)
Preston - Bolton (*Stagecoach 125*)

FANTASY BUS ROUTES

The Goggin (*Herefordshire*) to Giddy Green (*Dorset*)

WestwardHo! (*Devon*) to Pity Me (*Durham*)

No Man's Heath (*Cheshire*) to No Man's Land (*Cornwall*)

Locking Stumps (*Cheshire*)
to Solomon's Tump (*Gloucestershire*)

Bourton-On-The-Water (*Gloucestershire*)
to Spital In The Street (*Lincolnshire*)

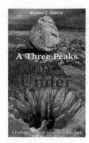

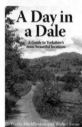

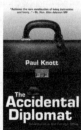

Also by Dave Hadfield

Dave Hadfield's seventh book about rugby league is devoted to one of the sport's great untold stories.

Learning Curve: The Remarkable Story of Student RL tells of how Oxford and Cambridge were conquered - places the sceptics said the game would never reach. It covers the development of 13-a-side rugby in the universities of England, Wales, Scotland and Ireland, as well as Australia, France and New Zealand. Student World Cups, Ashes series and thriving domestic comps are also featured, along with the author's inimitable and witty observations on the state of play today.

From dozens of interviews with those most closely involved, league's best-loved writer captures the spirit and dedication of the elite level, plus the humour of the lower echelons. Whether you played at university or college or not, *Learning Curve* is an unmissable treat for those who care about the future of rugby league.

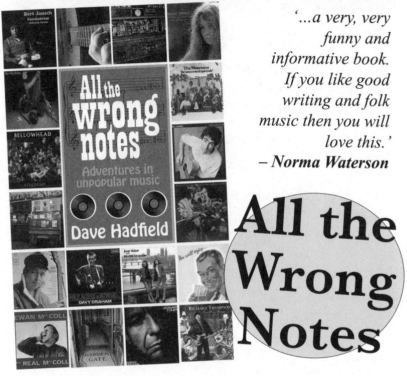

Adventures in Unpopular Music
By Dave Hadfield

For almost 50 years, Dave Hadfield has followed the genres of music that grabbed his youthful heart and mind. Now, in ALL THE WRONG NOTES, he has written not just a musical memoir, but a personal and social history of the last half-century. Like a Zelig with a finger in his ear, he has been where folk music has happened and describes it, affectionately but warts-and-all, in a way it has never been described before.

Hadfield's sure ear for quirks and eccentricities produces unique takes on major figures like Bob Dylan, Ewan MacColl and Leonard Cohen. It celebrates the foot-soldiers and their role in keeping left-field music alive. Humorous and provocative in equal measure, ALL THE WRONG NOTES is the key to a fascinating world of music.

Investigate our other titles and
stay up to date with all our latest releases at
www.scratchingshedpublishing.co.uk

85   rows   + 1 row to pick up

86   rows   6 buttons
- 12   rows   ←   = 2 rows
———   = 12 row
74

= 4 rows for beginning

= 70 rows ÷ 5 spaces   —
                           — 1
                           — 2
= 14 rows   — 3
                           —
                           — 4
                           — 5
= 4 rows   —
  2 rows
——————
6 rows   +   16 = 14 +2
              ∧ 5
             ———
             80 = 86 rows